# Vegetable Growing

# VEGETABLE GROWING

S. C. DEY

*Agrobios (India)*

*Dedicated to*
**Shri Ashis Dey**

*Published by:*
**Agrobios (India)**
Behind Nasrani Cinema
Chopasani Road, Jodhpur 342 002
Phone: 0291-2643993, Fax: 0291-642319



ISBN (HB) : 978-81-7754-011-6
ISBN (PB) : 978-81-7754-268-4



*Published by* **Agrobios (India)**, Jodhpur
*Lasertypeset at* Yashee Computers, Jodhpur
*Cover design by* Reena
*Printed at* Babloo Offset, Jodhpur

# Preface

The Indians are mainly vegetarian. India today has earmarked its vegetable production just to surpass any other country of the world. At present in India vegetables are grown in five million hectares of land and the production rises to 50 million tonnes per annum. India is the second largest country in the production of vegetable, still the per capita consumption is comperatively small. Hence more production is needed to cope with the demand.

The garden-fresh vegetables are more crisp and tasty than those which are sold by the green grocers. The fresh vegetables have more vitamins. Therefore, every house owner should have a kitchen garden to get fresh vegetable. Growing vegetable in home gardens has a special charm with a joy of creation. Generally, the housewives are more interested in kitchen gardening. The attraction of the fresh vegetables from one's own garden excites interest in gardening.

Growing vegetable is comparatively easy. It takes less time than growing cereals. In the context of these aspects, vegetable growing should be increased to replace cereal in our dietary to some extent. Many people take to growing vegetables in view of more financial gain. The present book will provide up to date knowledge and will develop interest in general public for growing vegetable.

I am grateful to those who have extended their help in preparing the manuscript especially with the photographs. If the readers find it useful, the efforts of all who are involved in bringing out the book will be fruitful.

Horticultural Arena
Jhargram, 721507

**S. C. DEY**

# Contents

# *Introduction*

Quantitatively vegetable ranks after rice and wheat in our dietary. It, like fruit, supplies us vitamins and minerals. The tuberous and root vegetables are also the sources of carbohydrates like rice and wheat. The main sources of protein being milk, meat, egg etc. Beans and pulses are the vegetable sources of protein. Fats have also both animal and vegetable sources. In this context I an not hesitant to remark that the variety of vegetables can supply us all the food elements we need both qualitatively and quantitatively. Secondly the vegetable contains plenty of fibre which are hardly found in other food article excepting whole wheat (*atta*). Fibre has important role in preventing many deadly diseases which is discussed in the appendix A.

Both fruit and vegetable supply us vitamins and minerals in the main. For the obvious reasons vegetables are more cheaply available than fruits. Therefore we have to depend more on vegetable than on fruit. Secondly fruit juice cannot supply us fibre that we need in quantities.

Both generic and specific variations in vegetables are numerous. Most of them, however, are the chooser of the climatic and soil conditions. Due to the recent advances in the plant breeding science innumerable cultivars of each vegetable species have been originated in this country. And much more are being imported from other countries. The main characteristics of the new being high yielding with the disease resistant qualities which ensure more production with less plant protection measures. Previously the most vegetables were season-bound, i.e. their production were seasonal. But the new breeding technique has enabled to originate competant varieties for the year-round production. Radish, bottle gourd, bitter gourd etc. are cited for example. The twenty six agricultural universities together with the vegetable research stations under the auspices of Indian Council of Agricultural Research have a landmark in the sphere of originating innumerable varieties suitable for our climatic conditions. Some reputed enterprieses have also undertaken vegetable breeding and attained a significant success that contributes largely to a sizeable production of vegetable and seed of the country. This is however imperative for growing food for the millions.

India today has earmarked its vegetable production just to surpass any other country of the world. At present it is being 50 million tonnes per year. The green vegetables are more perishable than fruits. Vegetables, like fruits. need to be preserved to prevent wastage through spoilage. So the high level of production envisages a plan for exporting fresh vegetables as well as the preserves. In the peak period a production especially in winter and spring exceeds much more than what is actually consumed. A popular proverb `Eat what you can and can what you cannot' should be the slogan to face the crisis of vegetable shortage. If the surplus vegetables are canned to preserve for the lean period the shortage can be counteracted by preventing wastage.

The quality vegetables have a great demand in the urban markets both at home and abroad, and fetch a high price.

All the vegetable species dealt with herein have been classified scientifically to make their generic relations conspicuous and to show the likeness in their cultural operations.

Vegetables are grown in the large fields, backyards of the houses where fruit trees are not grown and in the small kitchen garden of 100 square metre or so. The pot growers practically have no garden space. Generally they grow vegetable on the front terraces or roof tops. The book is designed to cover the aspects involved in these type of culture.

To reinforce the text a good number of figures and photographs have been reproduced. Although the subject being a branch of agriculture the language used in free from the technical terms, that makes the literature understandable to one and all.

Seventy three species of vegetable comprising the tropical and temperate, have been discussed to make the book exhaustive and more useful to the growers than any other work of this category.

# *Why Vegetable?*

The garden-fresh vegetables are more crisp and tasty than those which are sold by the green grocers. The fresh vegetables have more vitamins. So every house owner should have a kitchen garden or it becomes difficult to have the supply of fresh vegetable. Secondly growing vegetable in home gardens has a special charm with a joy of creation. Generally the housewives become more interested in kitchen gardening. The attraction of the fresh vegetables from one's own garden excites interest in gardening.

India being the second largest country in the production of vegetable. Still the per capita consumption is comperatively small. Hence more production is needed to cope with the demand. Secondly the quality production suitable for exporting and canning is however less than that of the developed countries. But the competent varieties for quality production are not wanting in this country. AT present in India vegetables are grown in five million hectares of land and the production rises to 50 million tonnes per annum. By this quantity of production the per capita consumption cannot rise above 125 grams per day. But the people of the developed countries consume at least 200 grams of green vegetables which obviously excludes vegetables like potato, sweet potato, yam, taro etc. To meet our deficiency we need more production of 10 million tonnes. In the beginning of the next millenium our vegetable requirements will rise to 83 million tonne per annum.

In view of the rapid population increase of the world the demand of the staple food (wheat and rice) increases tremondously. As its production cannot cope with the demand the sources of supplementary food has to be explored. Reasonably we first aim at the vegetables especially the tuberous crops. And at the same time we need to change our food habit. i.e. taking more vegetable than cereals (wheat. rice etc.)

Growing vegetable is comparatively easy. It takes less time than growing cereals. In the context of these aspects vegetable growing should be increased to replace cereal in our dietary to some extent. Many people take to growing vegetables in view of more financial gain.

A grower can grow vegetable through all the seasons of the year. But in case of cereals it is not easy. In the lean period of production especially in summer and in the rains the price of vegetable rises high. So the growers can make a sizeable profit due to the heavy demand. For our balanced nutrition we need plenty of vitamins and minerals. We get them easily and rather cheaply from vegetables. The normal growth and strength of the body as well as fertility are due to the presence of vitamin A in our food. It also develop resistance to cold and increase the eye sight. Lettuce, spinach (*palak*), cabbage, pea, tomato, carrot etc. contain vitamine A. To brace up the nervous system as well as the digestive system vitamin B-Complex is needed in plenty. It increases the appetile and can cure beri-beri. Beans or pod vegetables supply us protein along with enough Vitamin B-complex.

What we need more is Vitamin C. It removes the gum disease, prevents scurvy and activates the veins and arteries. Its deficiency causes articular pain at bone joints, which is usually confused with the gout. Vegetables lose much of their vitamin C content if fried in the cooking process. So green or boiled vegetables supply us plenty of vitamin C. Beans, cabbage, carrot, tomato, peas, potato, spinach and green chillies contain vitamin C in quantities. Vitamin D strengthens the bones. Its roles in removing ricket and dental disease are very important. Almost in all vegetables vitamin D is present.

Vitamin E removes sterility. All green vegetables especially lettuce contain this vitamin. For the normal growth of our body at least ten kinds of minerals are required. Of them most important are iron and calcium. Leafy vegetables, like amaranthus, fenugreek, spinach (*palak*)-contain enough calcium. The flowers of *Agasti* (*Sesbania grandiflora*) is preferred as a vegetable for calcium. There are other vegetables like carrot, bitter gourd, onion, tomato, fig. green banana etc. which contain enough iron. The rare element like iodine is available in onion, okra, squash, asparagus and teasle gourd.

The Indians are mainly vegetarian, because the quantity of animal protein in their diets is insufficient in comparison with those of the developed countries. So if we fail to produce vegetable much more than what is at present our national progress will be impeded.

# *Soil and Its Fertility*

The longitudinal section of the globe shows the presence of some distinct layers. The soil of the surface layer is somewhat blakish in colour due to the presence of humus, the decomposed organic substances. For this reason it is suitable for agricultural purposes. The subsoil is composed of many chemical substances instead of humus. The term `soil' is strickly applied to the layer of the earth surface which is not deeper than 30 cm. Because this layer contains the food elements suitable for the plant growth. The continuous use of a land for plant growing makes it more useful for agricultural purposes. Because the cultural operations along with the addition of the organic residues in the forms of decomposed roots, leaves, fruits, flowers, seeds and the waste matters from the animal bodies make it more fertile.

## MINERAL INGREDIENTS OF SOIL

The soil sample on examination reveals that it is composed of inorganic or mineral substances of various shapes and sizes. The sand particles through millions of years remains unchanged, whereas certain minerals are reacted and transformed into silicate clay particles and iron oxides in course of time. The amount of the mineral particles present in a soil determines its properties.

## ORGANIC SUBSTANCES OF SOIL

The animal and plants being the sources of organic residues of a soil. The plant parts and animal wastes are mixed with the soil on decomposition. Although small the organic residues contribute to the properties of the soil to a great extent. The organic residues bind the mineral particles for granulation that improves the soil structure. The plants get nitrogen, phosphorous and sulphur mostly through the organic matters. Humus increases the moisture retentivity of a soil.

## FOOD ELEMENTS IN THE SOIL

The plant foods in the soil remain in two forms which are soluble or insoluble. The complex food elements are changed to the soluble forms through the chemical or organo-chemical processes. Sometimes the simple soluble compounds can be changed into insoluble complex forms. The most of the soluble substances are absorbed by the plants and the rest is leached out thus going beyond the root zone. Besides nitrogen and carbon escape from the soil in the gaseous forms as nitrogen and carbon dioxide respectively. The soil testing should not only determine the quantity of the soluble elements and also those remain insoluble. The most of nitrogen, sulphur and phosphorous content of the soil exists in organic consistence. Organic nitrogen and sulphur become soluble more readily than inorganic phosphorous. Potassium, calcium and magnesium remains mainly in the mineral forms.

The following table shows the quantity of plant food contained in the soil of the different parts of the country (Review of Soil Research in India Part I 1982).

| Place | pH | Organic carbon (%) | Nitrogen (N%) | Potash ($K_2O$%) | Phosphorous ($P_2O_5$%) |
|---|---|---|---|---|---|
| Chinsura (W.B.) | 6.7 | 0.82 | 0.03 | 2.1 | 0.14 |
| Dighipura (W.B.) | 7.5 | 0.32 | 0.03 | 1.8 | 0.15 |
| Bhagalpur (Bihar) | 7.4 | 0.97 | 0.03 | 2.59 | 0.24 |
| Champaran (Bihar) | 8.7 | 0.51 | 0.04 | 9.00 | 0.21 |
| Pusa (Bihar) | 9.1 | 0.49 | 0.05 | 3.2 | 0.21 |
| Ranchi (Bihar) | 6.4 | 0.76 | 0.02 | 0.37 | 0.02 |
| Bhubaneswar (Orissa) Laterite | 5.6 | 0.36 | 0.35 | 1.55 | 0.45 |

| Place | pH | Organic carbon (%) | Nitrogen (N%) | Potash ($K_2O$%) | Phosphorous ($P_2O_5$%) |
|---|---|---|---|---|---|
| Bhubaneswar Alluvium | 6.3 | 0.81 | 0.03 | 0.9 | 0.05 |
| Meheburnagár (A.P.) | 6.75 | 0.53 | 0.06 | 2.71 | 0.05 |
| Hyderabad (A.P.) | 8.0 | 1.04 | 0.05 | 2.48 | 0.14 |
| Coimbatore (T.N.) | 8.3 | 0.4 | 0.06 | 1.82 | 0.32 |
| Tanjavoor (T.N.) | 6.6 | 0.17 | 0.03 | 0.58 | 0.04 |
| Trivandrum (Kerala) | 4.8 | 0.47 | 0.04 | 0.26 | 0.05 |
| Anand (Raj.) | 7.2 | 0.98 | 0.02 | 6.9 | 0.07 |
| Meerut (U.P.) | 10.2 | 0.52 | 0.04 | 3.43 | 0.08 |
| Garwal (U.P.) | 4.7 | 0.75 | 0.04 | 3.12 | 0.08 |
| Bilaspur (M.P.) | 6.7 | 0.4 | 0.06 | 4.1 | 0.29 |
| Karnal | 7.1 | 1.3 | 0.05 | 0.5 | 0.04 |
| Delhi | 8.0 | 0.45 | 0.03 | 2.16 | 0.30 |
| Jalandhar (Punjab) | 7.2 | 0.27 | 0.05 | 0.82 | 0.12 |
| Pune (Maharastra) | 7.6 | 0.73 | 0.07 | 1.9 | 0.21 |

## SOIL CONSTITUENTS

The basic soil constituents are three- clay, silt and sand. Their quantity differs in the different soils i.e. the ratio of their quantities are not the same in the soils of different locations or region.

### Soil Texture

A loan consists of clay, silt and sand in varying proportions. Clay and sand lie in the opposite poles so far as the textural value they impart to the loam is concerned. Because clay makes the soil heavy whereas sand makes it light. A heavy loam with its more clay content is sticky and light loam is friable. A medium loam, which contains both sand and clay in equal proportions is good for growing most vegetables. A clayey loam is bad for water penetration. Hence the drainage of excess water through percolation is not possible. On the other hand a light loam because of its more sand content cannot hold moisture for a long time. Silt is a substance lying between clay and sand. It is a sort of quartzic material. Clay is fine-textured, because the clay particles are very fine. The sand particles being coarse and as such add coarseness to the texture of a loam. The air space in a fine textured soil is very inadequate. For this reason soil aeration, which is so essential for garden plants is very poor in heavy soils. On the other hand, a light soil with plenty of sand particles is porous. For this reason soil aeration takes place satisfactorily.

## Soil Humus

Plant residues form humus. Leaves barks, roots etc. on decomposition turn into humus. Other organic substances of animal origin like dung, faeces, flesh, hides etc. on decomposition form a substance like humus. An agricultural soil contains humus. A soil without humus cannot be regarded as an agricultural soil. The plant residues that remain in the soil after cropping or seasonal weed growth add to the humus content of the soil.

For intensive agricultural purposes more humus has to be added to the soil with fertilizer. For vegetable growing the humus content of the soil must be high. Leafmould, leafmould compost, farmyard manure, green manure cow manure etc. are the sources of humus that can be used with advantage as a basal dressing during soil preparation as well as top dressing for supplementary feeding. Those soils devoid of humus must be improved first by green manuring successively (See `Green manure').

## Soil Structure

A soil or compost of improved structure is highly suitable for root growth. The friable and granular structure of a soil is considered to be an improved condition which is achieved by adding sufficient quantities of humus to it. For adding humus to the soil compost, leafmould, farmyard manure or cow manure is used. For potting compost or seed compost leafmould is considered to be the best source of humus. If leafmould is not available farmyard manure or cow manure can be used instead. The soil structure of a heavy soil (clay) can also be improved by adding lime. The grenulation of a soil facilitates aeration and drainage.

# *Manures and Fertilizers*

## PLANT FOOD

Plants take some elements as food for their growth and development from the soil and atmosphere. Those elements are nitrogen, phosphorous, sulphur, potassium, calcium and magnesium as well as iron, manganese, sodium, chlorine and silicon. There are a few more elements which are required in traces. They are copper, molybdenum, zinc, boron, etc.

These elements however cannot be utilised in their original form. They form the selective compounds which are absorbed by the plants. For example, nitrogen, which constitutes four-fifth parts of the atmosphere, cannot be utilized unless it is compounded with oxygen as nitrate or with hydrogen as ammonia to form a plant food. Similarly, plants use phosphorous as phosphates and potassium, calcium and magnesium as their salts. All these chemical compounds which plants absorb and utilize for their growth are regarded as plant food. Later we shall see that these compounds are available in different substances which are used as manures or fertilizers for plants.

The food elements are absorbed with water from soil. In nature any soil may contain plant food in considerable amounts, a fraction of which remains in an available form at a time. Because a plant cannot absorb the food elements unless they remain in solution, the major portion of plant food remains in an insoluble form in the soil. Plants cannot absorb concentrated plant food from the soil. If the concentration of food solution increases the plant's life will be at stake. Therefore one should be careful in applying concentrated fertilizers so that the chemical concentration does not reach a harmful level.

Plants need nitrogen, phosphorous and potash in large amounts. Hence they are called the BIG THREE.

1. **Nitrogen:** The vegetative parts visible to us are mainly due to the presence of nitrogen. The deep green colour of foliage, the considerable size of leaves and internodes, and a first growing condition indicate the sufficiency of nitrogen in the soil. If nitrogen is absorbed in excess compared to phosphorous and potash the growth will become shappy and this condition makes the plant susceptible to fungous diseases and causes delay in flowering and fruiting. When nitrogen is deficient the leaves become light green in colour and their size smaller.

2. **Phosphorous:** It can balance the sappy or soft growth caused by the excess of nitrogen. It also helps hasten flowering and fruiting and cause the remarkable resistance to diseases. Phosphorous is needed immensely to correct the succulent growth made by nitrogen alone. Early woody growth and early maturity indicate that plenty of phosphorous is present in the soil. If there is a deficiency of phosphorous the growth is retarded and the leaves become pale green in colour.

3. **Patassium:** It is indispensable for a well balanced and vigorous growth of a plant. In a potash deficient soil the quality of the products- flowers, fruits and tubers - cannot be high. Potassium is very helpful to enhance the disease resistant quality and saves plants from the drought. The deficiency symptom is manifested in drying up of the margin of leaves.

## OTHER ELEMENTS

Calcium is indispensable for the good growth of a plant, it helps in absorbing nutrients from the soil by the roots. Besides it performs many important functions in the plant body. Plants get calcium from lime.

Magnesium makes the leaves glossy green. Magnesium, like nitrogen, is leached out from the soil easily. Hence the deficiency of the element is a common occurance. It can be replenished by using epsom salt (Magnesium sulphate, ($MgSO_4$).

A deficiency of iron causes poor colouring of flowers and yellowing of leaves. Iron sulphate ($FeSO_4$) is applied to the soil to remove the iron deficiency in plants.

Boron is a very important element for growing good quality vegetable especially those are flowers heads like cauliflow, brocoli etc. It helps preserve tubers in storage. The tubers and bulbs grown by the plants enjoying the required amount of boron have a longer life and timely sprouting.

Generally, our soils are not deficient in boron. Its deficiency is likely to occur in an alkaline soil when boric acid ($H_3BO_3$) should be applied at a rate of 3 grams per litre of water. It must be noted that boron, even in a slight overdose will kill the plants. The role of other elements like copper, chlorine, manganese etc. does not seem to be so important in vegetables.

## SOURCES OF PLANT FOOD

**Manure:** Many substances, Manure both organic and inorganic, are used as manures and fertilizers to feed plants.

All organic matters, dead or excreted or obtained as wastes, when decomposed can supply plant nutrients. Therefore organic matters must undergo decomposition before it can be used as a manure. Leaves, barks, twigs, fruit peels, seeds, straws and grasses become manure on decomposition. But hoof and horn, leather, bone if pulverised, can be applied to soil. Similarly dry fish can be a good manure, oil-seeds after oil extraction, form a cake which is regarded as manure.

**Cow manure:** dung from many other animals is also used as cow manure on decomposition. Fresh, partly decomposed dung or dung cake which is used as fuel should not be used as manure. To prepare manure dung should be heaped in a pit which should be protected from dry or excessive moist conditions. When a pile of dung turns into manure it will be black in colour and its structure will be friable and granular.

A good cow manure is the best moisture retaining substance containing good humus. Besides nitrogen it contains 0.05 per cent of potash. This nutritional value will be two fold if the manure is prepared with great care giving it protection against sun and shower. The quality, however, will depend on the substance fed to the animal and the age of the manure. Cow manure may contain weed seeds in a viable condition.

**Poultry manure:** A good manure can be obtained from the faeces of domestic birds like ducks, fowls, pigeons etc. The faeces should be collected and piled in a moist condition for a year for decomposition. Poultry manure being rich in nutrients should be used carefully.

**Fish meal :** It is a good manure the use of which is common in pot plants. Dry fish in a pulverised form can be directly used as a manure. It can also be used in a friable condition on decomposition. In the kitchen garden especially in pot culture fish meal is used for a good result. A good fishmeal contains 5-7 per cent of nitrogen, 4-6 percent of phosphate and 4-6 percent of calcium.

**Compost:** Generally compost or farmyard manure is prepared from dung, urine, straw, vegetable wastes etc. compost can be a good substitute for cow manure. Water hyacinth, hedge clippings, other leafy garden refuse together with dung and urine can be the ingredients for making a good compost. They take a long time to be decomposed like cowmanure.

**Green manuring:** Green manure is obtained from green plants directly grown in the field which has to be manured. The seeds of a green manure crop (*Sesbania cannabina*) are sown as usual on the eve of the monsoon. So cannabina (*Dhaincha*) thrives well in a moderately rich soil. Before sowing apply supper phosphate at the rate of 100 grams per square metre. Obviously, the seedlings should grow thickly (300-500/sq.m). Just at the flowering stage strike down the green plants by rolling an iron drum over them. Then plough the soil thoroughly to mix the plant parts with the soil for decomposition. At a month's interval repeat the ploughing for mixing them intimately. After the rains when the moisture level of the soil is lowered remarkably the field should be prepared for planting. Green manuring increases the humus content of the soil. As the green manuring plants are the legumes (Plants of the pea family) the elemental nitrogen from the atmosphere is added to the soil by them. Therefore the green manure enhances the nitrogen content of the soil directly as well as indirectly. If the green manuring is followed by the application of chemical fertilizers during cultivation the optimal growth and production can be obtained.

**Oilcake:** The cake after extraction of oil from oil-seed is also used as manure, mustard, *neem*, castor and groundnut cakes are considered best. The use of mustard cake is very popular in the form of liquid manure. *Neem* cake in a dry or moist condition crumbles easily. Oilcakes in the pulverised form are used as basal dressing during soil preparation.

Until these get decomposed in the soil planting should not be done. After their application keep the soil in a moist condition for four weeks before planting.

**Hoof and Horn meal:** It is a good nitrogenous manure. It is usually mistaken for phosphatic fertilizer like bonemeal. Generally, nitrogen, if obtained from an organic or inorganic sources, is exhausted rapidly. Therefore it should be applied in split doses. But hoof and horn meal being a slow acting manure can supply nitrogen for a long period. In other words, it releases nitrogen slowly. For this reason its nitrogen is not wasted. It contains 13 per cent of nitrogen. If the substance is not pulverised well it will take time to release the nutrients.

**Leafmould:** Decomposed leaves form leafmould, Generally, the leaves of large deciduous trees are collected in late winter and stored in a moist condition for decomposition. Care should be taken to save the leaves from white ants. Leaves may take more than a year to turn into manure. A good leafmould is black in colour and friable in structure. Leafmould is a must for making potting compost. The pot grower of vegetable should use it for a good result.

Leafmould is a good source of humus. The quality of a leafmould depends on the kinds of leaves and the process of decomposition. It contains only one per cent of nitrogen. But its phosphate, potash and calcium contents are considerable.

**Bonemeal:** Cattle bones are mechanically ground to prepare bonemeal. Although organic it is treated as a concentrated phosphatic fertilizer. Bones also contain some gelatine which adds 4 per cent of nitrogen to the fertilizer. Bonemeal contains 20 per cent of phosphate.

**Bloodmeal:** It is a good nitrogenous manure which is used to improve the quality of pot vegetable. It contains 12-14 per cent of nitrogen and traces of calcium, sodium, potassium and phosphorous compounds Clotted blood from the slaughterhouse is collected and boiled for hours. Then it is dried and pulverised to prepare bloodmeal.

**Wood ash:** The white ash of hard wood contains 5-15 per cent of pure potash. Besides calcium, few other plant nutrients are also available. Wood ash is used as a manure to supply mainly potash.

## FERTILISERS

Many chemical substances contain plant nutrients. Certain compounds are however commercially manufactured in bulk for use as fertilizers. Such products are urea, super phosphate, muriate of potash, calcium ammonium nitrate (CAN), Potassium sulphate, etc. In this country the use of chemical fertilizers has increased. The remarkable results are obtained in growth and production when fertilizers are used with plenty of organic manures.

**Urea:** It is a concentrated nitrogenous fertiliser which contains only nitrogen and nothing else. It can be used as the basal dressing as well as top dressing or liquid manure for the growing plants.

Urea mixed with water can be applied as liquid manure of foliar spray. Two grams of urea is mixed with a little of water for spraying on foliage to remove nitrogen deficiency to some extent.

**Ammonium Sulphate:** Plants obtain 21 per cent of nitrogen from this fertilizer. It also supplies sulphur. Before the introduction of urea this fertilizer was the main source of nitrogen for plants in a chemical form. Now its use is very limited but it is highly recommended for alkaline soils ; because alkalinity is reduced by its acid reaction. Obviously, it should not be used in acid soils.

**Calcium Ammonium Nitrate:** It is also known as `CAN'. It contains 20 per cent of nitrogen and is used as basal dressing as well as top dressing.

**Di-Ammonium Phosphate:** It contains 18 per cent of nitrogen and 48 per cent of phosphate. Its abbreviated name is `DAP'.

**Super Phosphate**: It contains phosphorous penta oxide ($P_2O_5$) from which plants get phosphorous. Phosphate is not leached out from the soil with rain or irrigation water. It is of two kinds-single or tripple super phosphate. Single super Phosphate contains 16-18 per cent of phosphate and 19 per cent of calcium.

**Rock Phosphate:** This type of phosphate has been found in many rocks of India. Two rock phosphates - `Musouri Phos' and `Purulia Phos' are marketed as fertilizers.

Their nutrient contents are as follows :

Phosphate ($P_2O_5$)........................................ 20-24%
Calcium........................................................ 37-45%
Magnesium.................................................... 4-7%
Sulphur ........................................................ 4%
Zinc ............................................................. 100-150 P.P.M.
Copper ......................................................... 10-59 P.P.M.
Boron ........................................................... a trace

Rock phosphate is very useful for acid soils. Because it contains more calcium. Its phosphates becomes soluble only in acids. Therefore it should not be used in alkaline soils.

**Muriate of Potash:** It contains 80-85 per cent of potassium chloride and 15-20 per cent of common salt. Its potash content is high.

**Sulphate of Potash:** It contains 50-54 per cent of pure potash ($K_2O$). It becomes easily soluble in water and is readily absorbed by plants, and not easily leached out from the soil. Sulphate of potash, which is produced in India is used as a laboratory chemical. For its use as a fertilizer it is imported from other countries. For growing quality tobacco, sulphate of potash is essential. For this reason the whole of the imported material is distributed in the tobacco growing area. For having a heavy crop of quality tomato sulphate of potash is indispensable.

| Sources of other Nutrients | | (%) |
|---|---|---|
| Calcium | Limestone | 40 |
| | Quick lime | 71 |
| | Slaked lime | 54 |
| | Plaster of Paris | 23 |
| | Super phosphate | 19 |
| | Dolomite (a form of lime) | 30 |
| Magnesium | Dolomite | 21 |
| | Magnesium sulphate (Mg sulf or Epson salt) | 20 |
| Sulphur | Ammonium sulphate | 24 |
| | Gypsum (Plaster of Parish) | 18 |
| | Super phosphate | 8-13 |
| Boron | Borax (*Sohaga*) | 11 |
| | Boric Acid | 14 |
| Iron | Iron sulphates | 20 |
| Manganese | Manganese sulphate | 36 |
| | Manganous oxide | 77 |
| Molybdenum | Sodium molibdate | 36 |
| Zinc | Zinc sulphate | 36 |
| | Zinc Oxide | 79 |

Nutrient Content of Fertilizers

| | |
|---|---|
| 1 kg. nitrogen is available from | 5 kg. of Ammonium sulphate, 1200g of urea or 4 kg. of CAN or 3840g of Ammonium chloride. |
| 1 kg. phosphate is available from | 6250g of Single super phosphate or 3 kg. of Triple super phosphate. |
| 1 kg. Potash is available from | 2 kg. of Muriate of Potash or Sulphate of potash. |

## COMPOUND FERTILIZERS

The compound fertilizers are prepared to supply a number of major nutrients from a single product. The name of the product is suffixed with some figures indicating the percentage of the nutrient contents. For example, Suphala 15:15:15 means $N_{15}P_{15}K_{15}$. In other words one kilogram of Suphala contains 15 per cent of nitrogen ($NO_3$), 15 per cent of Phosporic acid ($P_2O_5$) and 15 per cent of potassium oxide ($K_2O$). But Suphala 20:20 does not contain potash. It has only 20 per cent of nitrate and the same amount of phosphoric acid. If you want to get 1 kg. of nitrate, 1 kg. of phosphoric acid and 1 kg. of potassium oxide, you have to use 6666 g of Suphala 15:15:15. But 5 kg. of Suphala 20:20 contains 1 kg of nitrate and 1 kg. of phosphoric acid. Similarly the analysis of Gromor 28:28:0 is N 28: P 28 : KO. So 280g of nitrate and 280g of phosphoric acid are available from 1 kg. of the product. The analysis of IFFCO 10:26:26 is N 10 : P 26 : K 26. So 100g of nitrate, 260g of phosphoric acid and 260g of potassium oxide are available from 1 kg of the product. Besides the products containing both organic and inorganic substances of nutritive value are also available in the market. Of them Sterameal and Rallimeal are popular. Their analyses are N7:P10:K5 and N6:P8:K5 respectively.

## MAINTAINING FERTILITY

The fertility status of a soil can be maintained with the practice of good soil management and judicious fertilizing with the balance use of organic and inorganic substances.

Maintaing good tilth and controlling weeds are the practices of soil management.

First remove the factors that causes soil erotion as well as those responsible for bad drainage. The use of more chemical fertilizer and proportionately less organic manures containing plenty of humus lowers the fertility status of the soil. If the organic residues decrease by degrees adopt green manuring by raising the green manuring crop and then treading, beating, ploughing and mixing it with the soil. It will add to the humus content of the soil, which increases the microbial activity in the soil. The microbes are considered the life of soil. The microb population will increase with the rise of humus content. The decomposition of organic matters in the soil is due to the microbial activities. The microbes change ammonia into nitrates and sulphur into sulphur dioxide. Thus adding fertility to the soil. The main functions of the soil microbes are nitrification, nitrogen fixation and sulphur oxidation. These are so vital that in absence of which the life of the higher plants and animals will be at stake.

The crop rotation helps maintain the fertility. A particular crop should not be grown in a plot continuously. But the legume crops are the exception. In the process of crop rotation one legume should be grown alternately. At least two other crops including one legume should be grown.

# *Soil Reaction*

A Soil may be acid, alkaline or neutral. There is a scale ranging from 1-14, which is known as ` $P^H$ scale'. The mid-point being 7 that indicates the neutral condition of the medium. The soil having $P^H$ above 5.5 is suitable for the normal microbial growth and activity. In lower $p^H$ aluminium, iron and manganese become soluble to a great extent and reach a toxic level. Hence harmful to plants. Comparatively in high $p^H$ these ions become soluble in lesser quantities which is considered enough for the plants. Even copper and Zinc become available in a $p^H$ around 7. But boron becomes insoluble. Hence unsuitable for many crops especially cauliflower, broccoli etc. When such problems arise the micronutrients should be fed through foliar feeding. Molybdenum becomes available in a higher $p^H$.

The role of acidity is very significant as regards the availability of phosphorous. Its ions always remain in an adsorbed condition with the soil coloids. When a soil pH remains at 6.5 strongly adsorbed phosphorous ions tend to be loose, i.e. the force of attraction is considerably reduced. In this condition the roots can get the phosphorous ions in exchange of hydrogen ions. When the alkalinity is increased considerably the carbonate ions increase that prevent the availability of other nutrient ions. To determine the fertility status of a soil the indirect effects of the soil reaction has to be considered.

To reduce acidity lime is used. The different types of lime are available in the market. They are limestone, Quicklime (calcium oxide), hydrated lime (Calcium hydroxide), chalk etc.

**Limestone:** Though chemically it is a form of calcium carbonate ($CaCO_3$) it also contains some quantities of magnesium carbonate ($MgCO_3$). Limestone is applied in a pulverised form at the rate of 300-400g per sq.m.

**Dolomite:** It is another form of limestone which contains 46 per cent of calcium carbonate and 43 percent of magnesium carbonate. So it can remove the deficiency of both calcium and magnesium. Dolomite is applied 150-300 per sq.m. of land.

**Quick lime:** Chemically it is calcium oxide.

When it absorbs moisture from the atmosphere it becomes hydrated lime and is used in lime concrete and white washing. Due to its caustic action it is not so easy to use in the soil. Scientifically it is said that its neutralizing power is 182.1. In other words in neutralizing acidity 100g of calcium oxide is equivalent to 182.1 g of calcium carbonate. To raise the pH 5.5 to 6.5 165-220 g of calcium oxide is required for a square metre of ground space.

**Chalk:** It is a form of calcium carbonate ($CaCO_3$). Finely ground chalk is applied at the rate of 100-300g per sq. metre.

**Use of lime:** To determine the correct amount of lime one should have the soil test report.

Lime in the carbonate form is very easy to apply. Lime in any form should be finaly ground. Calcium oxide when absorbs moisture crumbles to dust. After tilling and laddering lime is applied by sprinkling uniformly. After 2-4 weeks basal dressing of manure and fertilizer should be applied.

Hydrated lime has two forms- air -slaked and water slaked. That is why it is called `Slaked lime'. The air-slaked lime is used by sprinkling. For its caustic action it should not be used when the breeze is blowing.

# *Soil Preparation and Drainage*

## TILTH

Spading or ploughing is necessary to loosen the crusted soil. A dry soil becomes more rigid and this condition makes tilling difficult. The soil must be just moist to break evenly while ploughing. On the contrary if it is too wet it becomes sticky, a condition that cannot be made friable by ploughing. On tilling the moist soil becomes friable and granular which is suitable for handling soil for manuring, sowing, transplanting etc. To break the lumps of soil evenly laddering is done just after ploughing. In small plots however, the lumps are crumbled by beating them with a club-like wood-piece.

The depth of tilth is an important thing to consider. The surface soil up to the depth of 20-30 cm. is suitable for growing crops. Therefore tilling deeper than this layer of soil is useless, rather harmful. Almost all vegetable crops can be grown successfully in a tilth of 15-30cm. deep. The deep tilling lift the sub-soil which does not contain humus to the surface layer. On the other hand the fertile soil of the surface layer goes downwords, thereby making the top soil less fertile.

Tilling soil is done with the use of plough or spade. For tilling a small plot of land spading is convenient. Spading one spit deep is sufficient for growing vegetable.

After tilling humus or bulk manure is added by broadcasting evenly. Obviously the manure must be granular and friable. To make the texture uniformly granular seive the manure through 5-10mm. mesh before use. The fertilizer mix with balanced NPK may be added to the manure. On applying manure the land should be ploughed again to mix it with the tilth. To make it levelled laddering should follow. The application of manure or fertilizer or the both after tilling is known as `basal dressing'.

The next operation is to make the deep furrows at a regular distance, which have to be used for irrigation or drainage of surplus rain water. It is obvious that the furrows should run along the slope of the plot. The furrows should be 25cm. deep and parallel to each other. The distance between the two adjacent furrows should be one metre. This space is used to show seed or transplanting seedlings and for which a number of shallow furrows and low ridges are made crosswise. These ridges are made 30-45 cm. apart as required for the particular crop. Generally seeds are sown or seedlings are transplanted on the ridges, some times the seeds are sown or seedlings are transplanted in rows without making any ridge. Afterwards by earthing the rows of ridges are made. Thus between the ridges furrows are formed.

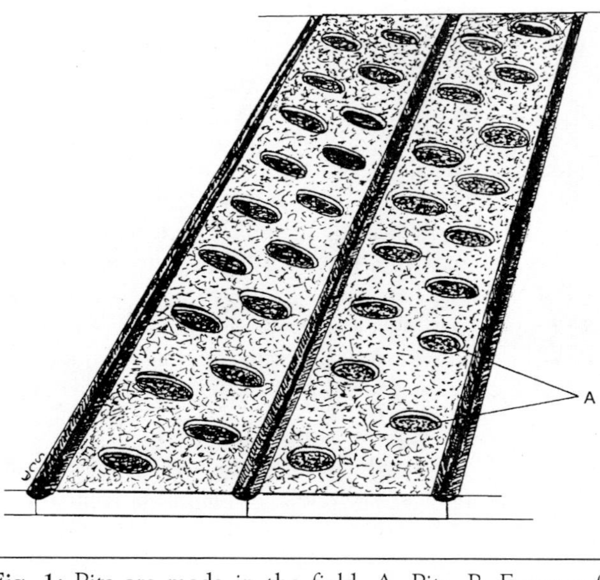


**Fig. 1:** Pits are made in the field. A. Pits, B. Furrows for irrigation or drainage

Some crops are grown in pits. Therefore instead of making ridges pits are made in which manure and fertilizer are used more in quantities. Because the cucurbits such as gourd, cucumber melons, ephalandra, momordica etc. grow long vines that need more space and feeding. Other creeping vegetables like sweet potato, yam etc. are grown in pits or basins. For growing large plants like vegetable, banana, papaya, elephant foot, giant taro etc. the pits of large dimensions are used. The spacing between the pits depends upon the spreading habit of the vine, i.e. week or short vines need less space to cover. The exact spacing for the individuals of the species or variety has been mentioned in that chapters dealing with them. The depth of a pot varies from 25-35 cm. its width 30-45 cm. The top of the pit should have the form of a basin that can hold irrigation water for percolation. For the *Kharif* crop in a heavy rainfall area the basins are filled up with soil or compost.

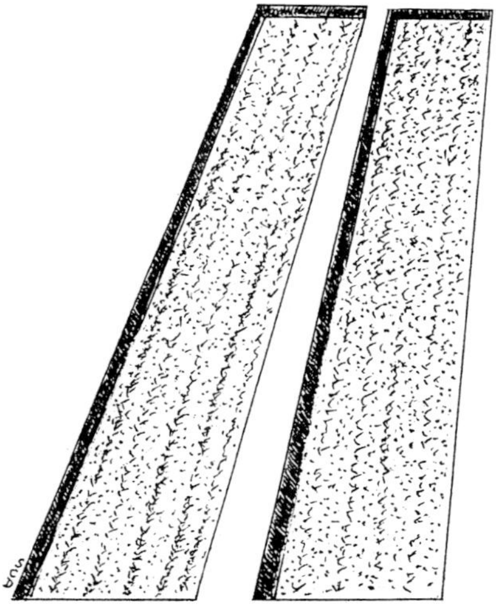

**Fig. 2:** Low beds for vegetable in *kharif*.

To drain out the surplus rain water the plot should have a gradual slope that should be 1 cm. per metre of the length. The deep furrows made during the soil preparation are connected with a ditch running crosswise in the lower level. It is obvious that the ditch should necessarily be deeper and wider as it runs to a distance. The ditch of the plot must be connected to the drainage channel of the locality. The following are the manure and fertilizer mixes for fertilizing the soil, any of which is used as a basal dressing. The different crops of vegetable need different ratio of NPK for their proper growth and optimal production. For this reason the N. P. K (the ratio of nitrogen, phosphorous and potash) has already been mentioned. In calculating N. P. K the contents of humus or humus-like substances that mainly improve the structure of the soil has not been considered. The total requirements of fertilizers are applied in split doses, especially that of nitrogen. Potash and phosphorous which are not leached out from the soil are usually applied as the basal dressing during the preparation of soil. The full requirement of nitrogen of the crop is usually used in three split doses. Therefore, one-thirds of the total quantity is added to the mixture for the basal dose which is applied while preparing the soil. For example, for growing brinjal in an acre of land the N, P, K requirement is 60 kg(N), 20kg(P) and 25kg(K). In the basal dressing only 20kg of nitrogen should be used. The ingredients of the mixtures are as follows. Humus (Leafmould/ compost /Farmyard manure) 50-70 tonne/acre

Urea ........................................................ 44 kg.
Super phosphate ........................................ 122 kg
Muriate of Potash ...................................... 50 kg

Or

Humus........................................................ 50-70 tne/acre
Oil cake (Pulverised) ................................ 225 kg.
D.A.P. ........................................................ 42 kg
Muriate of Potash ...................................... 50 kg

When Oil cake is used transplanting should be done 3 weeks after the preparation of soil. In the mean time the soil should remain in a moist condition so that oil cake gets decomposed and becomes manure.

For growing tomato N.P.K requirement is 30:20:30. In case of tomato the total N.P.K should be applied as basal dressing during soil preparation. In other words the supply of nitrogen need not be made in split doses. The fertilizer mixture for tomato should be as follows.

Humus........................................................ 48 tne/acre
Pulverised oil cake (Neem/mustard) .......... 200 kg.
D.A.P. ........................................................ 24 kg.
Urea ........................................................ 37 kg.
Sulphate of potash ...................................... 60 kg.

For the quality production sulphate of potash is preferable to muriate of potash. The ash obtained from burning tobacco stems can supply potash of a good quality. It is not however practicable for commercial culture. But it can be adopted in the kitchen garden or in pot culture.

Cauliflower has more fertilizer need. It is practically more than any other vegetable crop. Its N.P.K need is 60:30:30 For the basal dressing it should be 20:30:30. As such the mixture should contain the following ingredients.

Humus........................................................ 48 tne/acre
Oil cake...................................................... 350 kg.
D.A.P. ........................................................ 63 kg.
Muriate of Potash ...................................... 65 kg.

(Oil cake needs to be decomposed to become manure. So transplant the seedlings 3 weeks after the preparation of soil).

OR

Humus........................................................ 48 tne/acre
Urea ........................................................... 40 kg.
Super phosphate ........................................ 170 kg.
Muriate of potash ...................................... 65 kg.

It is obvious that the different crops need nutrients in different quantities. So for them the soil will be prepared accordingly. The following table shows the nutrient requirements of different crops of vegetable.

| Crop | Nitrogen | Phosphate | Potash |
|---|---|---|---|
| Brinjal | 50 | 20 | 24 |
| Tomato | 30 | 20 | 30 |
| Cauliflower | 50-60 | 30 | 30 |
| Cabbage | 50-60 | 15 | 20 |
| Bottle gour, Ash gourd Pumpkin etc. | 24 | 20 | 15 |
| Ridge gourd, Parwal Bitter gourd etc. | 25 | 22 | 15 |
| Leafy vegetable | 30 | 25 | 25 |
| Knol-Khol | 30 | 20 | 20 |
| Beet, Carrot, Turnip | 25 | 20 | 30 |
| Pea | 10 | 25 | 25 |

| Crop | Nitrogen | Phosphate | Potash |
|---|---|---|---|
| Okra | 30 | 20 | 20 |
| Radish | 30 | 20 | 20 |
| Onion | 50 | 30 | 50 |
| Water melon and Muskmelon | 25 | 20 | 15 |
| Beans and Cow peas | 8 | 8 | 8 |

# *Raising Seedlings and Transplanting*

Generally seeds are not sown directly in the field. Seedlings are raised in the seed beds or seed pans. Then 2-4 week old seedlings are pricked out and transplanted on the ridges of the prepared soil of the field. The seeds of gourd, cucumber and leafy vegetables like spinach, amaranthus etc. are sown directly in the field. The seeds of brinjal, tomato, chilli, onion, cauliflower, cabbage etc. are sown in seed beds or seed pans, and then seedlings are pricked out for transplanting in the field.

## SEED BED

The soil of the seed bed should be a good loam having 50 per cent of clay and silt and fifty per cent of sand. In case it contains more clay add humus more in quantities. The necessary tilth should be 15 cm. deep. The soil structure must be friable and granular. It is better to spread a layer of seived soil of 5cm. deep on the bed.

Humus and phosphatic fertilizer will be mixed in the soil of the seed bed. Both humus and super phosphate are mixed thoroughly and seived through 5mm. mesh. Spread the mixture over the bed 2-3 cm. deep and rake into the soil upto 5 cm. depth. Generally in the seed bed nitrogen and potash fertilizers are not used. For nitrogen a light dressing of fine hoof and horn meal can be used. It has to be done 15 days before sowing seeds. As plenty of humus is used it removes the deficiency of nitrogen and potash necessary for the seedlings.

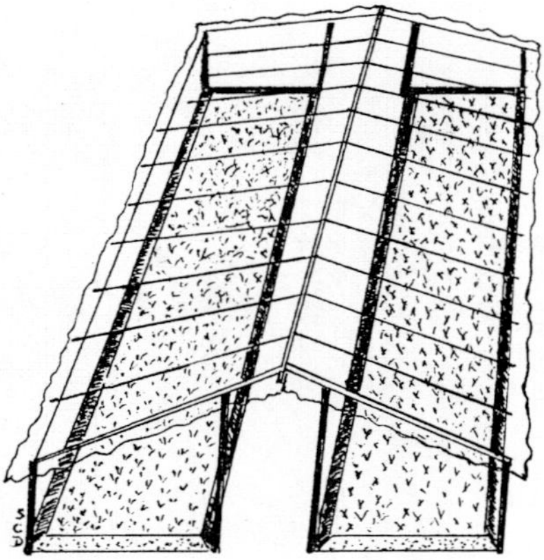

**Fig. 3:** Seeds beds under a poly-shed.

The seed bed should have an exposure to the sun at least for 8 hrs a day. The bed should be raised by 15-20 cm. from the adjoining land. It should have the protection from the strong sun and shower by putting an over shed. If the soil of the bed is not sterilized the germinating seeds may be destroyed by soil fungus. The insects like ants and mole crickets (*Gryllotalpa vulgaris*) may eat up the seeds sown in the bed. The top layer of the bed can easily be sterilized by drenching it with the formalin solution (See kitchen Gardening) To repel the insects like ants and crickets use B.H.C. powder or any substitute by dusting. Aldrin, D.D.T. etc. are common substitutes. The liquid termite killers like Darsban or Pyriban can keep the soil insects at bay. The snails and slugs may attack your seed bed. To ward off them dust finely powdered *Mahua* cake or granular insecticides around the seed bed.

The seeds are sown as usual i.e. they should be distributed evenly over the entire space. Then cover the seeds by sprinkling fine-grained cow manure or sand. The cover should not be thicker than the height of the seed laid over the bed. Then water the bed thoroughly with a water can fitted with its fine rose. On watering if the seeds are exposed at places then cover them again as before. Seeds before germination do not need light, direct or diffused. To keep them in the dark spread a thin layer of paddy or wheat straw over the bed. Some prefers to cover the seed bed with a sheet of black polythene. It can be done in a cold weather. But its use in a hot weather is definitely harmful to the germinating seeds. As soon as the germinated seeds raise their head the straw cover must be removed. Watering once a day is a usual practice. So long the beds have the straw cover they need less watering.

Seeds should not be sown thickly. Because the congested seedlings fall victim to the damping off disease. By this disease the portion of the seedlings just above the soil level rots. On incidence the unaffected seedlings should be removed and transplanted carefully and thinly in a new bed.Before pricking out spray the seed bed with copper fungicide like Blue copper or Blilox thoroughly. The seed for sowing per square metre is given below.

| Seed | Space | Quantity of seed |
|---|---|---|
| Cabbage | 1 sq.m. | 8 g |
| Cauliflower | | 8 g |
| Knolkhol | | 8 g |
| Brinjal | | 6 g |
| Tomato | | 6 g |
| Chilli | | 6 g |
| Onion | | 5 g |

Before sowing the seeds should be treated to kill the germs of the seed-borne diseases. To treat 1 kg. of seed 3 g of Agrosan G.N. or Serasan is required.

When the quantity of seed is small it should be sown in the seed pans. The shallow pots of burnt clay having 30 cm in diameter and 7 cm. depth are used as seed pans. After crocking the pots are filled with seed compost. The surface level of the compost should remain just below the rim. This empty space is necessary for holding water while watering. The following is the seed compost which can be used in the seed pans.

Medium loam.............................................. 5 buckets (10 litre cap.)
Humus........................................................ 2 L
Hoof and hornmeal (fine) .......................... 400 g.
Super Phosphate ........................................ 300 g.
Wood ash / muriate of potash .................... 300 g.

The process of sowing seed is the same as described for the seed bed. After sowing seeds the pots are placed under a shed until the seeds germinate.

It the deficiency of nitrogen is evident in the growing seedlings a little urea is mixed with a litre of water and applied with a water can after watering the bed or seed pan.

There is a practice of sowing the germinated seeds. For this seeds are soaked in water for 6-12 hrs., then put them in a gauze bag which is placed within a stack of compost for 2-3 days. Therein the high temperature is very conducieve to germination. Obviously the seeds should remain just in a moist condition. This practice is found feasible in winter when cold weather retards the germination of the seeds of summer vegetables. Just when the winter vegetables are over a great demand of summer crops are created. And the price level remains high for a month or so. For this reason the market growers like to raise the early crops. For this purpose they have to start right from December and January. The vegetables that need winter sowing are okra (Lady's finger). pumpkin, bottle gourd, bitter gourd, ridge gourd, cucumber, melon, *phuti* and *poi* etc.

Seed Treatment (See Chapter 20).

## TRANSPLANTING

When the seedlings of the seed bed or seed pan grow 4-6 leaves they become fit for transplanting in their permanent site of the field or kitchen garden. They are planted on the ridges prepared already. At the planting time the soil must be moist, for which it may need to be watered 10-12 hrs. before planting. It is better to transplant the seedlings in the afternoon. The pricked out seedlings will droop immediately if planted in the strong sun. In a cloudy day it can be done any time from the day break to sun down.

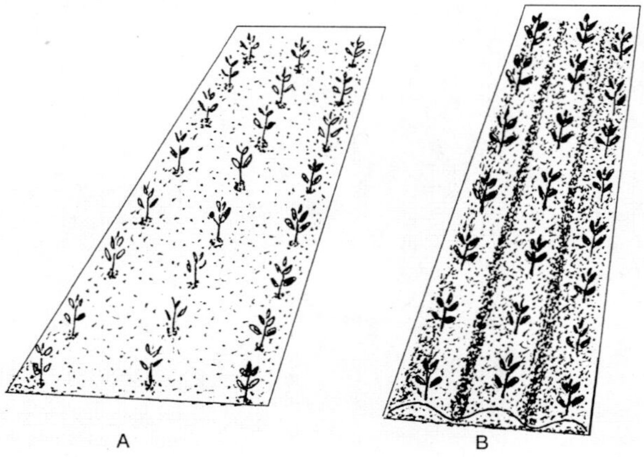


**Fig. 4:** Transplanting seedlings and making ridges. A. Seedlings are planted in the plain, B. As they grow ridges are made by earthing.

Care should be taken not to sever the roots considerably while pricking out. If the seed bed is prepared with plenty of humus the seedlings grow many fibrous roots that help them to stand transplanting. Mark the planting points at a regular distance fixed for species. Scoop out a little soil with a fork or trowel and plant one seedling in a hole as usual immediately after pricking out and water with a fine rose of the water can.

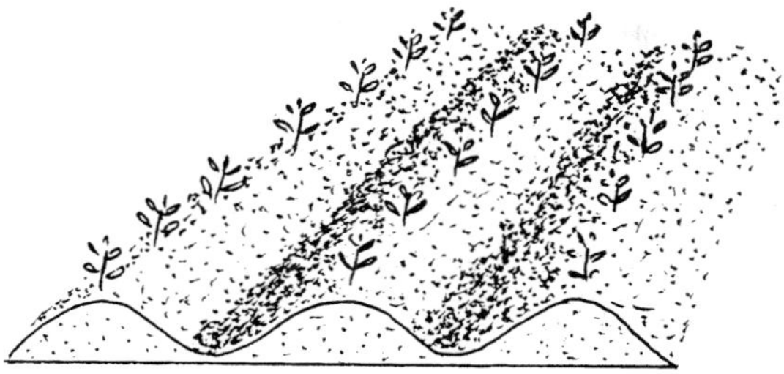

**Fig. 5:** Seedlings transplanted on ridges.

Next day if the sun becomes very strong the seedlings just planted may need protection from the scerching sun. The small flower pots or paper bags if placed inverted over the seedlings from 9 A.M. -4 P.M. can keep them in a comfortable shade. This may be repeated for the next day. Within two days the roots will take soil and start growing when they need the full exposure to the sun.

# *Cultural Operations*

## IRRIGATION

In our sub-tropical region the cultivation period has two main divisions, such as *kharif* and *rabi*. For the farmer no irrigation is required as there is plenty of showers at short intervals. In the later a prolonged dry spell prevails. Therefore irrigation at short intervals become essential. In late summer, i.e. in May-June nor-western showers are experienced, which occur usually at a weekly interval. The acute water scarcity is relieved to a great extent by these occasional showers. Sandy soils cannot retain moisture for a long period. Obviously it needs irrigation at a very short interval. So in *rabi* cultivation much more water is required for irrigating crops of the light soil.

**Sources of Water:** Fresh water is used to irrigate vegetables. In the coastal region brackish water is also used, which is slightly saline. Canals, marshes, ponds, lakes, rivers etc. serve as the sources of water for irrigation. The wells or tubewells (Shallow or deep) are now used extensively for the commercial culture of vegetable.

**Slope:** The natural slope of the plot is utilized for irrigation. If such slopes do not exist the earthwork is necessary to make the slant. One centimetre slope per metre is enough for this purpose. As water runs towards the slope the irrigation water must come from the upper level of the plot.

**Procedure:** The field of vegetables needs two types of irrigation, e.g. light irrigation and flow irrigation. On sowing seed or transplanting seedlings light irrigations are given. The water can, sprinkler, bucket-mug or any other light water container is used for this purpose. For a flow irrigation much more water is needed, and by it the soil to a depth get drenched thoroughly. First water is brought from the source to the main channel constructed along the highest line of the plot. Then it is allowed to pass through the deep furrows made at a distance of one metre in the plot. The flow of water should be such as to cover a width of one metre on either side of the furrow. The irrigation furrows are made along the slope of the plot. If the slope is not gentle water will run fast and reach the end before drenching the sides. It has already been said that a slope of 1 cm. per 1 m. form a gentle slant for irrigating the plot and draining off the surplus rain water. The water when running through the furrow the flow is obstracted at certain distances so that it can flow side-wards before overflowing the obstacles. The flow irrigation in a kitchen garden is usually done by a hose pipe connected to a pipe-line of the house.

## FEEDING

The growing plants are fed with the feed supplements when deficiency is likely to occur. Sometimes they are applied when the deficiency symptoms are observed. In growing vegetable at least nitrogen is applied in split doses. The full quantity of other major nutrients (Phosphorous and potash) is generally applied in the basal dressing. If their deficiency is observed they should be added to the feed supplements.

Supplementary feeding is done in two ways, e.g. by top dressing and liquid form. The former is applied by broadcasting at the top and raked into the soil. The second dose is applied in the line, which is followed by earthing up thus making ridges in the line of planting. Immediately after top dressing irrigation should be applied.

The manure in the liquid form is called liquid manure. The fertilizer ingredients which can be diluted in water are used to make a liquid manure. Both chemical and organic substances can be used in liquid manure. Urea, oilcake (mustard, groundnut etc.), muriate of potash, magnesium sulphate etc. are used in a liquid manure. To add phosphate fertilizer supper phosphate can be used. Then it should be soaked in water for a day or so before use. The following ingredients may be used to prepare liquid manure.

Oil cake (mustard or groundnut) ...............800 g

Urea.............................................................200 g

Sulphate of Potash ..................................... 80 g
Super phosphate......................................... 120 g
Magnesium sulphate ................................... 40 g.

Soak the oil cake in 10 1 of water for a week. Add other ingredients in 5 1 of water for 24 hrs. Then mix two liquids and add water to make the solution of 60 1.

Liquid manure is suitable for kitchen gardening and pot culture of vegetables. It is applied just after watering the plants. Sixty litres of liquid manure can be applied in 60-100 pots. In the ground it is applied in furrows of 100 m length. Liquid manure is very cheap and quick acting. It is however not convenient for the large-scale culture of vegetables.

## FOLIAR FEED

The plant can be fed through leaves. Certain nutrients cannot be absorbed by plants due to complex soil reactions. To avoid this trouble the nutrient solution is straightway applied to the leaves by spraying. Generally, the trace elements or micro-nutrients are fed through leaves. After a few days of application the plants will show the signs of sufficiency of the nutrients applied. The trace elements need not be applied more than twice in a seasonal crop.

Now-a-days, proprietary products which can be used as a foliar feed are available in the market. They should be used as per the directions of their manufacturers. A list of the popular products are given below.

| Products | Manufactures |
|---|---|
| Agromin | Arris Agrovet Industrial Products Ltd. Mumbai-43. |
| Tracel-2 | Rallis India, Bangalore-54 |
| Multiplex | Karnatak Agri Chemicals Bangalore -10. |
| Micronutrient Mix | Pausak Ltd., Baroda-3 |
| Plantarin | Kamdhenu Chemicals, Pune-2. |
| Vipul | Godrej, Boecy. |

### Hormone and Biostimulants

To prevent fruit drop in chilli, papaya etc. auxin in the form of proprietary product `Planofix' is applied twice or thrice by spraying on leaves at an interval of a week. Besides there are a good number of agro-chemicals which are known as `Biostimulants', They are applied by spraying on leaves. Now they are applied to grow more vegetable in the commercial field as well as kitchen garden. On spraying the plants grow healthy and yield early. The following is the list of some proprietary products.

| Products | Manufacturers |
|---|---|
| Miraculan | National Organic Chemical Products Ltd. |
| Aminos | Rallies India Ltd. |
| Sungrow | Herbinger Phytochemicals |
| Paras Photosynth | Hindustan Lever Ltd. |
| Biozyme | Wockhardt Ltd. |
| Arogen | Pharma-flora India. |

Any of the above products can be sprayed at an interval of 4 weeks. To increase the yield of cucurbits the following biostimulants are used. Ethral, M.H.-40, Tiba, Agrono, Bardhak, Citozime etc.

## HOEING AND WEEDING

Both the operations go hand in hand. The crusted layer of the top has to be broken for the aeration in soil and the percolation of irrigation water for the thorough soaking of the root zone.

Wheel hoe, rake, fork or *nirani* (weeder) is used to rake the soil. Hoeing loosen the hard soil of the top thereby facilitating weeding. Because the anchorage of the roots of the weeds become loose. Hoeing is done one or two days before irrigation. On hoeing eradicate and remove all the weeds.

In the *kharif* the irrigation is not usually needed but the weed growth becomes more rampant. As such though the cost of irrigation is saved in the rains the expense in weeding increases.

## MULCHING

The mulch is a cover on the soil surface to conserve moisture and to provide aeration that is needed by the feeder roots. In summer when water for irrigation is wanting the proper mulching saves the plants to a great extent.

Coarse manure, chopped or half dicomposed straw is usually used as the mulching materials. U.V. stabilized black polythene sheets are now available in the market for this purpose. The long strips of land between the two adjacent rows of plants are covered by the mulch. If polythene is used the strips are cut measuring the width and spread over the space. Coarse-grained cowmanure or compost is highly suitable for mulching. Hoeing is not necessary if mulch is applied. Because the soil below the mulch does not become crusted. The feed supplements in the form of top dressing or liquid manure are applied on the common mulch. But in case of polythene mulch it is removed for hoeing, feeding and watering, and replaced again after the operations.

## SUPPORT FOR CLIMBERS

The creepers and climbers need support for spreading their vines. All the cucurbits are climbing species. Besides some legumes (beans), yam, sweet potato, etc. are climbers. There are also some which have scandent or sub-scandent stems, e.g. Poi (*Basella* spp.), *Kalmi* (*Ipomoea reptans*), tomato etc. They prefer to spread prostrated on the ground. *Poi* has its very fleshy stems that may rot by the soil fungus. Therefore, *Poi* grown as a *kharif* crop should have a support for spreading so that the stems do not touch the ground. The vines of the *rabi* crop mostly spread trailing on the ground. But those in the rains spread better on the support vertical or horizonal. Week vines bearing large fruits as in the bottle gourd, pumpkin, melon etc. need ground support better than trellises or pergolas.

Wood slat or bamboo slats and branches, dry branches of bushy trees are used for giving supports. The wire nettings, welded or woven, are also used in the kitchen garden for this purpose.

The small vines grow upright. Hence vertical supports are provided. The heavy climbers first grow vertical then horizontal for which trellis or pergola is constructed. The trellis is fence-like structure of vertical bars and cross bars. Pergolas are like a canopy which are supported by a number of bamboo poles.

# *Cole Vegetables*

## CAULIFLOWER (*Brassica oleracea* var. *botrytis*)

**Family : Brassicaceae.**

**Other names : Hindi - Phoolgabhi, Beng. - Fulkopi. Guj. - Fulkobi, Tam. - Gospoovu.**

The most important vegetable of this class. In the plains of India it is available from September to February in the market. It sets seed in the hills where winter is long. The high quality seed is imported from the European countries.

The early varieties are grown in the rains especially in the hills. The mid-season varieties come to the market in early winter. The late varieties having their large heads are available in mid winter and continue till the middle of spring. Their curds (heads) are very white but become yellowish in spring. Because it is a cold weather crop. The seed of early varieties is sown in May-June in the northern plains, June and July in the southern plains and March - April in the hills. For early and late varieties 3 and 2 g of seed is required per 10 Sq.m. area respectively.

For the early varieties loam is suitable, and for the midseason and late varieties heavy loam is ideal. The soil should be of $p^H$ 5.5 - 6.5. The basal dressing of manure and fertilizer per acre is as follows.

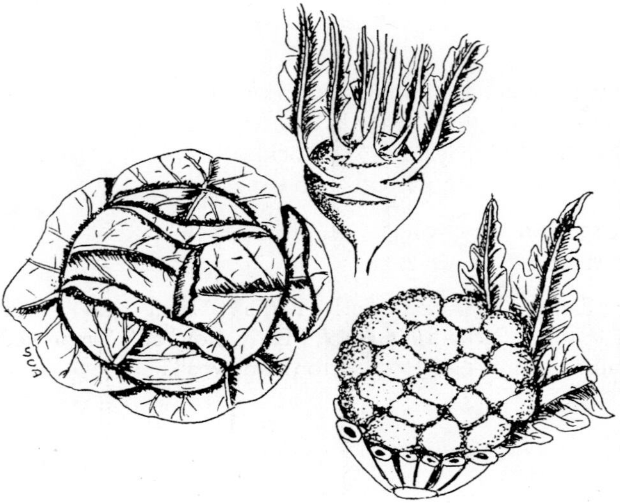

**Fig. 6:** Cole vegetables (Cabbage Knol-Knol and Cauliflower)

Humus (Cow manure/compost) ................ 48-72 tonne
Urea ........................................................ 50 kg.
Superphosphate ......................................... 80 kg.
Muriate of potash ...................................... 50 kg.

Before sowing the seeds should be treated to remove the disease infection. The seed rate is 250-300g for an acre of land. The seedling requirement is 15-18 thousand for the mid-season varieties and 10 thousand for the late variety. Seeds germinate within 3-4 days. 5-7 week-old seedlings are transplanted. The seedlings that become hard and remain stunted in the seed bed cannot produce a perfect curd. After three weeks of planting a ridge is formed in the line of planting by earthing thus making a furrow between the two adjacent rows. The furrows are used for irrigating and feeding. The first top dressing is applied on the ridges and earthing is done again thus making the ridges high. For top dressing 60 kg. of urea and 25 kg. of muriate of potash per acre are applied. The early varieties become ready within 60-70 days and the mid-season and late varieties within 90-120 days. The production per acre ranges from 70-75 quintals. To improve the quality of the curd the plants should be sprayed with foliar feed to remove the deficiency of micronutrients. The deficiency of boron mars the quality of the crop. Because the curds will not be compact and pure white and the stalks become hollow. Spray boric acid (3g/L) after 4 weeks of transplanting. Borox (*Sohaga*) can be used instead of boric acid. Borax is dissolved in hot water. First get it dissolved in a little water and then mix with the rest for spraying.

The black spot on leaves and wilting cause harm to the crop. So the seed treatment with fungicides as described in Chapter 20 is necessary.

**Varieties:** Early-`Kunware', `Early Patna', `Pusa Katki' Mid-Season - ``Aghani', Poosi, `Patna Main crop', `Early snowball', `Improved Japanese' Late - `Dania', `Snow-ball-16', `Sutton's Snowball'.

## CABBAGE (*Brassica oleracea* var *capitata*)

### Family : Brassicacae

Cabbage is a very tasty and nutritious vegetable. The popularity of the crop knows no bounds. The cultural technique is very similar to that of cauliflower. Cabbage, like cauliflower, has early and late varieties. The seedling requirement is 10-15 thousand per acre. Six-week-old seedlings are transplanted at a distance of 45cm x 50cm or 50cm x 75cm. Before starting the formation of head the crop requires more water. But Then it should be controlled, i.e. minimised afterwards. On head formation if the irrigation is not controlled the heads may burst. The early crop is harvested on 90 days and the late on 105-120 days. 10-15m. tonne yield per acre has been recorded. Although it is a cold weather crop. A very cold weather is not suitable for the rapid growth. Seed setting takes place in the cold weather of the hills.

**Varieties:** ***Round headed types:***`Golden Acre', `Pride of India', `Copenhagen Market', `Express Flat', Drumhead type - `Pusa Drumhead', ***Conical head type***: `Jersey Wakefield'. ***Savoy type***: `Chieftain' ***Chinese cabbage***: `Chihill', `Wong Bok', Pakchoi (non-heading).

## KNOL KHOL (*Brassica oleracia* var. *caulorapa*)

### Family : Brassicaceae

**Other names : Hindi - Ganth gobi ; Beng. - Olekapi, Guj. - Nolvol; Oriya & Assam - Olkobi, Tam. - Noolkhol.**

Knol-Khol is grown with ease. Though it is very nutritious not so popular in this country. It gives Vitamin A and B with plenty of carbohydrates.

The species is hardy and as such is grown easily. The planting and after care are the same as those of cauliflower. The seed rate is 2 kg. per acre of planting. The seedlings are transplanted 25cm. x 30 cm. (Plant x row) apart. The stem just above the ground swells to become globular which is used as vegetable. The crop becomes ready in 90 days. With the age the globular base (Knob) becomes bulky and stiff and strong fibres develop thus indicating the edible stage is over. The crop at the tender stage is used as vegetable. When this stage is over it is fit for feeding the cattle. An acre of land can yield 7.5 - 10 tonne. Knol-Khol does not set seed in the plains.

**Varieties:** `White Vienna', `Purple Vienna', `King of North', `Kholrabi', `King of Market'.

## BRUSSELS SPROUTS (*Brassica deracea* var. *zenker*)

### Family : Brassicaceae

**Other names:** ***Eng.*** **`Bud Bearing',** ***Beng.*** **- Chokenapi',** ***Tam.*** **- `Marakkhose'.**

Brussels sprouts is a native of Brussel of Belgium. Hence the name. The small cabbage like heads sprout on the stem of 60cm. high. It is mainly grown on the hills as it needs long winter. 250 g of seed has to be sown for an acre of land. 10cm. high seedlings should be transplanted at a distance of 50cm x 50cm (plant x row). Fertilizer requirements are like that of cabbage.

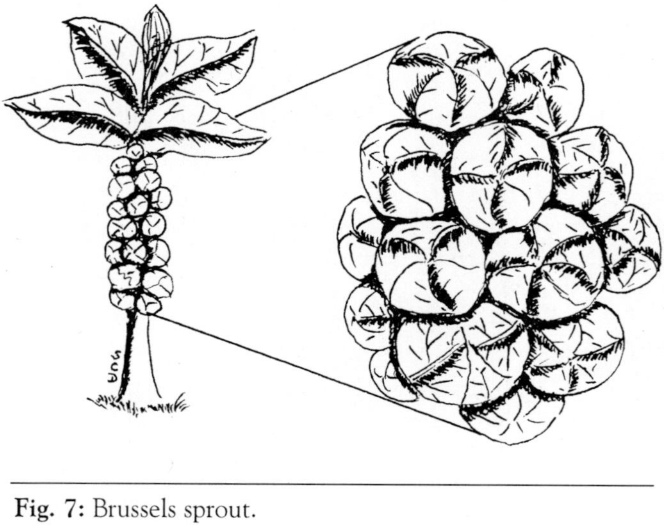

**Fig. 7:** Brussels sprout.

Top dressings should be applied just at the age of 3 weeks and 7 weeks. A well fed plant can produce 20-40 heads. The head of the top should be nipped in the bud that help grow the lateral heads.

**Varieties:** `Catskill', `Long Island', `Danish Prize', `Hilds Ideal', `Express' etc.

## SPROUTING BROCCOLI (*Brassica oleracea* var. *italica*)

### Family : Brassicaceae

**Other names : Beng. - `Dalkopi, Eng. - `Green cauliflower',**

Broccoli supplies vegetable for a long time. Because the lateral shoots also bear flower heads, though smaller than the terminal head. As the flower is green it is also called `Green Cauliflower'.

**Fig. 8:** Broccoli with a number of flower heads.

The cultural technique is The same as that of cauliflower. So long in India it was grown in the kitchen garden only. But now its popularity has grown and the culture has been taken up commercially. The seedlings are transplanted at a distance of 75cm x 75cm. (Plant x row). When the terminal head begins to open it should be cut with a stalk of 20-25 cm. The lateral sprouts will also be cut in the like manner. The sprouts should be sent to the market immediately or they will turn yelllowish green.

**Varieties:** `Calabrese', `Bronzino', `Italian sprouting'.

## KALE (*Brassica oleracea* var. *acephala*)

### Family : Brassicaceae

The plants resembles cabbage but the head is not formed. In other words the leaves remain loose, they grow wrinkled and look very ornamental. For this reason it is also an object of the ornamental garden. Its leaves are cooked as vegetable. It is more nutritious than cabbage.

**Fig. 9:** Kale

It contains protein and vitamin A,B & C. The growing technique is the same as that of cabbage. Kale does not thrive above 21°C. It prefers a slightly alkaline soil. In America kale is a crop of lesser importance. Still in its one State (Virginia) kale of 15 millions of rupees are produced annually.

Kale has three different colours - green, white and purple. On the basis of their origin Kales are also known as Scoch or Siberian kale.

# *Legume Vegetables*

Beans, peas, cowpeas etc. belong to the family of *Leguminosae*, The members of this family produce seed pods and develop nitrogen nodules on the roots. Rhizobium bacteria take shelter in the nodules, which can fix free nitrogen of the atmosphere for their host plants. For this reason legumes are grown for fixing nitrogen in the soil. In the process of crop rotation legumes have a great role in restoring fertility of the soil. If the soil contains sufficient phosphates and potash the nodule formation is increased thus making nitrogen fixation more in quantity.

## FRENCH BEAN (*Phaseolus valgaris*)

### Family : Leguminosae

**Other names: Hindi-Bakla, Frash bean, Rajmah (seed); Beng.-Faras seem; Guj.-Phanasi; Tel.-Bariglu.**

Franch beans have two types - one for the plains and the other for the hills. On the basis of the plant size it has two types, e.g. Bushy and climbing.

French beans are grown early and pod setting takes place within 40 days of sowing seed. One of the reasons of its popularity is the habit of early bearing. For kitchen gardening or pot culture French bean is a must. The varieties of the hilly areas are found to be delicate in the plains. French beans contain plenty of protein. The vegetable also contains calcium, iron and vitamin A.

Seed is shown just before winter. When a field is first utilised with French bean becteria innoculation should be incorporated for the better growth of nitrifying bacteria that help increase the yield. For an acre of land 9-12 kg. of seed is required. Seeds are sown 10 cm. apart in the rows. The gap between the rows should be 30-45 cm. The weak seedlings are removed. The top dressing with 15 kg. of urea is applied per acre after 3 weeks of sowing seed. Then earthing is done to make ridges in the rows. For higher yields the foliar feeding is adopted at an interval of 10 days until the plants decline. Provide stakes or support for the runner or pole-type varieties.

Aphids attack the crop very often. Anthracnose, mildews, rust, wilting also may attack. The control is given in Chapter 20.

**Varieties:** `Contender', `Giant Stringless', `Pusa Parvati', `Tendergreen', `Kentucky wonder' (Pole-type), `Earliest of All', `Darjeeling Premier', Masterpiece', `The Prince', `Sprite', `French White', `V.P.F.-191' etc.

## PEA (*Pisum sativum*)

## Family : Leguminosae

**Other names: Sans. - *Satila,* Hindi - *Matar,* Beng.-*Matar, Karai Sunti*; Guj.-*Watani*; Tam.- & Mal.-*Pattani*.**

Pea is a pulse, but in the green stage it is a popular vegetable. It is rich in protein, vitamins and minerals. Loam, especially alluvium is highly suitable for growing pea. It does not prefer an acid soil. The soil $p^H$ 6-6.5 is ideal. If first grown the soil should be mixed with the bacteria innoculation. Seeds are sown 10-15cm. apart just before winter. There are innumerable varieties of pea. The size and shape of the pods of the different varieties are not the same. The taste also differs. In the hills it is grown all the year round.

Before sowing seeds should be treated with Dithane M-45. Seeds are sown on the low ridges. On top dressing and earthing the ridges will be high. The plants is scandent but like a climber They have trendrils at the leaf apex. If the support like a trellis is provided the plants grow vertically. The weak seedlings should be removed at the early stage. On flowering apply a top dressing of urea at the rate of 15 kg. per acre.

Aphids, pod borer and anthracnose may attack the crop.

## DOLICHOS BEAN (*Dolichos lablab*)

### Family : Leguminosae

**Other names:** Hindi - Sem, Beng. - Shim; Guj. -Val; Mar.-Pavla; Tel.-Chikkudu; Mal.-Avara.

It is also known as `Field Bean'. It is a very common and popular bean. It has many varieties, most of them are flat. One of them is `Moture' meaning pea-like. Both the pod and seed resemble those of pea. Another variety `Hatican' is long (15-20 cm) and flat. Dolichos beans are of two types, one is suitable for the field and the other for kitchen gardens. The field beans are now extensively grown in Karnatak, Tamil Nadu, Andhra Pradesh and Madhya Pradesh. The garden variety bears only in winter. It needs support for climbing and spreading. Healthy seedlings should be raised 3 m. apart in July - August. 2-3 treated seeds should be sown in a pit. After two weeks retain only one which is strong and growing fast, and remove the others. It starts flowering from October when top dressing should be applied. Top dressing of 15g of urea and 10 g of muriate of potash is recommended at a month interval.

The disease and pest control is as recommended for French bean.

## LIMA BEAN (*Phaseolus lunatus*)

### Family : Leguninosae

**Other names: Hindi - *Sem*, Tam. -*Khasi Kollus* ; Punjab-*Lobiya*; Eng. - Butter bean.**

It is very delicious with high protein content. Pods are fleshy which is borne in a cluster of 5-6. Seeds are sown in pits at a distance of one metre in September - October in the plains. One healthy seedling should be retained per pit. The plants are made bushy by pinching the top at the age of 45 days. The fruit setting starts at the age of 70-75 days. If the flowers drop without fruit setting help them to open by cutting the tips of the opening bud. Then cross pollination and fertilization would take place. It is very popular in America, but not liked by many in this country.

**Varieties:** `Florida Butter', `Challenge', `Burpee', `Burpee's Bush', `Henderson Bush' etc.

## COWPEA (*Vinga unguiculata* syn. *V. sinensis*)

### Family : Leguminosae

**Other names:** Sans.-*Nisapava,* Hindi- *Lobia,* Beng.-*Barbati,* Guj.-*Chorap,* Mar.-*Chaoli;* Tam.-*Karamanti.*

Cowpea is a very common and popular vegetable. It is grown all over the country. Its weak trailing stems need support for climbing and spreading. It climbs up the support by twining. Its long pods hang in clusters. There is an old variety which grow trailing on the ground and holds the stalk of the flower bunch much above the ground so that the pods do not touch the ground. Cowpea is a very delicious and protein-rich vegetable.

Cowpea has both summer and autumn varieties. The former is grown during summer and the rains, and the later bears from September to November. For the summer crop sow seeds in February and the monsoon crop, in April-May. The seedlings of the autum crop are raised in July - August.

Seeds are sown in pits one metre apart. Only two strong seedlings are retained per pit. Feeding is like that of French beans. On flowering apply top dressing thrice at an interval of three weeks. Cowpea, like French bean, is shallow rooted. Hence more irrigation is needed in dry and hot weather. The plants cannot stand water-logging.

Like pea the ripe seeds are a sort of pulse. `Rajmah' is one of them.

**Varieties:** `Pusa Phalguni' (for summer), `Pusa Barsati' (for rainy season), `Pusa Dofasali' (for both seasons), `Early Philipin'.

# *Cucurbits*

The species belong to the family *cucurbitaceae*. As many as 25 vegetables are cucurbits. They are mainly summer crops. In other words they are found less in winter. The large ripe fruits of pumpkin though grown in hot weathers can be stored for the winter use.

All these species grow weak trailing stems. But they have trendrils to climb up the support. Mostly fruits and in some cases leaves also are used as vegetable. From small fruits of cephalandra, bitter gourd and parwal to the giant fruits of bottle gourd, pumpkin and ash gourd are available in cucurbits. All the cucurbits have male and female flowers either on the same plant or on the different. Parwal, teasle gourd etc. bear male and female flowers on the different plants.

## PUMPKIN (*Cucurbita maxima*)

### Family : Cucurbitaceae

Other names: Eng.-Red gourd, Hindi-Lalkumra, Mitha Kumra', Beng.-Lal Kumra, Misti Kumra; Tam.-Parangikayi; Mal.-Mathan.

Pumpkin contains plenty of potassium and vitamin A & B. 100g of fruit contains as much as 339 mg. of potassium. It is grown in all parts of the country. It has many varieties which are suitable for different seasons of the year. The fruit shape and size also differ in the seasonal crops. A fruit may weigh 1 kg-30kg. In a kitchen garden where there is no plenty of sun shine red gourds can be grown with success. In course of four months crop can be harvested. It is a quick growing heavy creeper. The large -fruited varieties are grown to spread on the ground.

Seeds are sown in pits which are at a distance of 2m. When the vines begin to spread top dressing should be applied in the entire plot. Because the nodes (leaf joints) of the stems send out adventitious roots and absorb nutrients.

4-5 seeds are sown 2-3 cm. deep per pit. Of them two healthy seedlings are retained per pit. For the *Kharif* crop sow seed in April-May, for the *rabi* it is to be done in January-February and for winter cropping raise the seedlings in September - October. Gourd needs more potash and phosphate fertilizers. Nitrogen should be applied in three split doses. If more nitrogen is applied in the beginning the vegetative growth will be increased at the cost of fruit bearing. Gourd prefers top dressing of oil cake just when pistillate flowers (female flowers) appear. For the *rabi* crop the irrigation should be regular so that the field does not run dry. Pumpkin has large leaves which completely cover the ground thus controlling weed growth. The *Kharif* crop is raised cheaply because the cost of irrigation and weeding are practically minimum. For the top dressing the quantity and the ratio of nitrogen and potash should be determined on the basis of plant growth and fruit setting. If potash is wanting the taste of the vegetable will be insipid.

Generally the bees visit only the male flowers for collecting pollen. So pollination does not take place as the female flowers remain unvisited. Therefore hand pollination is necessary, which should be done just before visiting of the bees.

Red pumpkin beetles eat up the leaves of the tender plants. Fruit flies damage the tender fruits especially of *kharif* crop. Mosaic virus may be a menace to pumpkin culture.

**Varieties:** `Arka Chandan', `Coimbatore-1', `Coimbatore-2' `Pusa Biswas', `C.M-14', `Large Red', `Baidyabati' etc.

## BOTTLE GOURD (*Lagenaria siceraria*)

### Family : Cucurbitaceae

**Other names: Sans.-*Alabu*; Hindi-*Kaddu, Lauki* ; Beng.-*Lau*; Guj.-*Dudhi tumada*; Tam.-*Shorakkai*; Punjabi-*Ghiya*;**

Bottle gourd is a vegetable of all seasons. Both fruits and vines are consumed. The round, long and extremely cylindrical-fruited varieties are available. But they are seasonal. It, like pumpkin, has small, medium and large-fruited varieties.

The varieties should be selected according to the season. The seed should be sown as stated for pumpkin. But those are grown for the summer crop their fruiting can be extended up to July. 1 kg seed is required for an acre of land. Pits are prepared 3 m. apart, 4-5 seeds are sown per pit. Two healthy seedlings are retained per pit. The plants are quick growing and the vines run fast. When the fruit setting decreases the vines are cut, put into bundles and sent to the market as a pot herb. Some grows it for only the tender shoots. They apply more nitrogen that makes the vines grow at the cost of fruiting. Top dressings are applied at a month interval in the pits. As the stems do not develop roots top dressing should not be applied in the rest of the field.

**Varieties:** `Pusa Summer Prolific Long', `Pusa Summer Prolific Round', `Pusa Mighdut; `Pusa Manjari', `Pusa Navin', `Punjab Komal' etc.

## CUCUMBER (*Cucumis sativas*)

### Family : Cucurbitaceae

**Other names: Sans.-*Sukasa*, Hindi. Bengali & Mar. - *Khira*; Tel.-Dosakaya; Tam.-*Kakrikai*.**

Cucumber is a very nutritious and popular vegetable, 100g of it contains 9 mg. of vitamin C. The green fruits are eaten fresh and ripe ones are cooked to consume. It is grown in plenty in summer and the rains. The cold tolerant varieties have also been introduced, which yield in winter. For the early crop the germinated seeds are sown in winter so that the fruit can be obtained from early or mid spring.

Alluvival loam is ideal for cucumber. Heavy soil with plenty of added humus is also suitable for a good yield.

Seeds are sown in pits which are made 2 m. apart in rows. The gap between the rows is 1 m. 2-4 seedlings are raised per pit. The top dressings are applied only in the pit at an interval of four weeks. 20g of urea or 40 g of ammonium sulphate is applied per pit as top dressing. The tender fruits are plucked that fetch the better price. Other details of culture and pest and disease control are the same as for pumpain.

**Varieties:** `Poinset' (American), `Poona khira', `Balam Khira', `Khira-75' `Khira-90', `Japanese Long Green' `Straight-8' `Pusa Sanjog', `Priya', `Super Slicer', `White Wonder', `Improved Long Green' etc.

## SQUASH (*Cucurbita moschata*)

### Family : Cucurbitaceae

**Other names: Eng. - `Vegetable marrow'; Beng.-`*Bileti Kumro'***

Quash is a vegetable of hilly regions. It hardly grows well in the plains. Its tender leaves, vines, flowers, fruits and roots are used as vegetables. Fruits contain enough Vitamin C. Its vines are short. Some varieties are bushy. Fruits are small and the duration of bearing is more than that of pumpkin. The fruits are small. In shape and size they resemble papaya to great extent.

**Fig. 10:** Squash

Pits are made 1m apart. Seeds are sown in winter or in the rains. 2-3 seedlings per pit are retained. The growing technique is the same as for pumpkin. The fruit setting starts after 60 days of sowing.

**Varieties:** `Early Yellow Prolific', `Australian Green', `Butternut' etc.

## ROUND GOURD (*Citrullus vulgaris*)

### Family : Cucurbitaceae

**Other name : Hindi-Tinda.**

Round gourd is one of our idigenous vegetables. It is mainly grown in the northern parts of the country. It contains vitamin-A in plenty. It is preferred most for its cooling effect. Very hot climate and light alluvial loam are required for growing round gourd.

The seedlings are raised in pits in rows from February-June. 2-3 seedlings are retained per pit. For each pit 12 sq.m. of space is allotted for spreading the vines. The furrows between the rows are used for irrigation or draining off surplus rain water. The top dressing is applied as in gourd. Irrigation should be frequent for the *rabi* crops. The fruit setting starts when vine begins to run. The tender fruits are picked. The fruits as long remain tender retain soft hairs as in ash gourd. If tender fruits are plucked the plants bear more. It is delicious so long its seeds are soft. The yield per acre runs from 3000-4000 kg.

Varieties: `Arka Tinda', `L.S. -48' etc.

## POINTED GOURD (*Trichosanthes dioica*)

### Family : Cucurbitaceae

**Other names: Sans.-*Putulika*; Hindi-*Parwal*; Beng.-*Patal*; Mal.-*Palalam*.**

Parwal is one of the best summer vegetables. It is easy to digest and nutritious. Iron, calcium, Potassium and vitamin (A & C) rich parwal are available for 8 months in the market.

Alluvial loam of the river side or river basin is ideal for growing parwal. The plant is grown from the fleshy roots, vines, vine cuttings or seeds. Seed germinates well still it is not preferred by the growers. The seed propagation is used mainly for breeding purposes or originating new varieties through selection. The seeds of ripe fruits are collected and sown immediately which germinate within 1-2 weeks. The plants grown from seed yield fruits of different size and shape. Hence not preferred by the market growers. The large percentage of seedlings become male.

The roots or vines are planted in pits of rich soil in October-November. The mature vines of 2m long is twined to form a ring of 25 cm. diameter, which is planted horizentally 3-4 cm. below the surface of the pit. The roots of finger thickness are suitable for planting. 2-3 roots should be planted vertically in a pit. The crown should remain 2 cm. below the soil level. Both the roots and vine rings should be treated with fungicides before planting. On planting the pits is mulched with coarse cow manure or compost. It helps conserve moisture and prevent baking of the top soil if exposed to sun and air. By watering keep the soil of the pit moist. Within a month the crown of the roots or the nodes of the vine ring will sprout roots and shoots.

In parwal male and female flowers are borne on two different plants. So for pollination and good fruit setting the male plants should be planted in the field. In a plot of one acre 10-15 male plants (distributed evenly) should be there.

After the land preparation the pits are made and manured as usual. When the vines begin to spread the field should be irrigated. The top dressing are applied from April onwards at an interval of one month. The top dressing is applied both in the pits and the rest of the field as in pumpkin. For each dressing 100g of powdered oil cake and 20g of muriate of potash should be applied in each pit. If humus and fertilizer mixture are not applied during soil preparation it should be when the vines begin to spread. Parwal, like pumpkin, prefers top dressing with oil cake. As humus is mixed as the basal dressing in top dressing only fertilizer mixture is applied.

Powdered oil cake ...................................... 50 kg.
(Neem/mustard/ground nut)

Urea ............................................................ 15 kg.

Muriate of potash ...................................... 5 kg.

This mixture is for an acre of land. It is obvious that the *rabi* crop needs irrigation frequently. If nor-wester and pre-monsoon showers are normal irrigation is needed less. In light soil the yield increase in the rains. Though no irrigation is required the weed growth becomes heavy that entails much expense in weeding.

Practically no pest can cause any harm to the crop. But the fungous disease damages the leaves, stems and fruits. Fungicides should be sprayed regularly at an interval of 10-15 days especially in the rains.

The field once planted lasts for three years. In November all the vines are cut and removed. The roots with their crowns should be retained. On sprouting new shoots from crowns the field should be tilled by spading. In the first year the plants were only in the pits, but in the second and third years the roots grown from the nodes of the vines cover the entire field. The thicker roots sprout shoots in winter. If their numbers are too great thinning should be done to maintain a distance of 50-60 cm. between them. The surplus roots can be planted in the new field or sold to the new growers. The top dressing and irrigation should be started from the first week of February.

The plants grown in the river basins are destroyed by the flood water in the rains. In such cases new planting in October becomes necessary.

**Varieties:** `Dandli', `Kalyani' `Guli', `Bihar Sarif', `Sopari Safeda', `Niria', `Santokhia', `Damodar', `Kajli', `Ghughut Bombai', `Amra Banti' etc.

## BITTER GOURD (*Momordica charantia*)

### Family : Cucurbitaceae

**Other names: Hindi-*Karela,* Beng.-*Karela,* Mar.-*Karle.* Kan.-*Hagal.* Mal.-*Kaippa.***

Bitter gourd is a bitter vegetable that contains vitamin A & C and the minerals like potassium and magnesium. Though bitter in taste still it is very popular. Its price in the market is also high. Through all seasons it is available. But in winter its production becomes less and becomes high in spring and in the rains. Both large and very small fruited varieties are there.

In the *rabi* crop vines are allowed to cover the ground but in the rains the stakes or supports are provided to climb. The large-fruited varieties even of the *rabi* crop should be given stakes to grow vertically. Otherwise the long fruits will get a curve. The seed requirement is 1 kg. per acre. The pits are prepared 150cm. apart. 3-5 seeds are sown per pit.

Ultimately 2 strongest seedlings are selected and retained for growing. On fruit setting 20 g of urea is used as top dressing per pit at an interval of two weeks. For the *rabi* crop two irrigations are needed per month in heavy soils. But the light soil area needs more irrigation, i.e. once a week. Under the shade of a pergola of bitter gourd the soil does not get direct sunlight. So it does not dry up quickly. So less irrigation is required. The yield per acre varies from 30-60 quintals.

The pest and disease control is the same as recommended for gourd.

**Varieties:** `Pusa Domousmi', `Kalianpur', `Baramasi', `Coimbatore White Long', `N.D.B.-1', `Punjab B.G.-14'.

## TEASLE GOURD (*Momordica dioica*)

### Family : Cucurbitaceae

**Other names: Hindi-*Kaksa;* Beng.-*Ban-Karela, Kankrol,* Tel.-*Agakara;* Assam-*Bhatka Karela.***

Teasle gourd is rich in protein. iodine and vitamin C. It has small, medium and large fruited varieties. It is found to grow in the semi-forest or fallow lands. Now it is cultivated in the fields and kitchen gardens. The fruits are heavily seeded, i.e. not so fleshy but very nutritious. Its root is tuberous and the separate plants bear male and female flowers. For pollination and fruit setting the presence of male plant at least at a ratio of one male plant per 100 female plants is necessary.

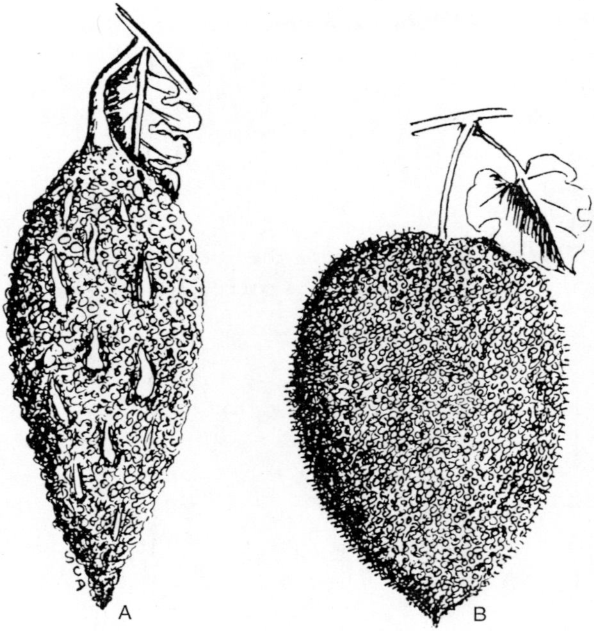


**Fig. 11:** Two cucurbit. A. Bitter gourd B. Teasle gourd

The plants are grown from seed or tuberous roots. The tubers remain dormant in winter and sprout in summer. The seeds dispersed from the ripe fruits of the plants germinate and grow to seedlings all around in May-June.

The cultural technique is the same as for parwal. It, however, unlike parwal, does not send out adventitious roots from the nodes. So each plant grow only one tuber. Teasle gourds require stakes or supports for climbing and spreading of the vines. The sprouted tubers are planted in pits 1m apart in March-April. The seedlings grown in seed pans are transplanted in June and July just on the eve of monsoon.

A plant can bear for 5-6 years. In November the vines dry out. Then they should be removed. The fleshy roots may remain in the field or dug out for stroing. The plant can also be propagated by shoot cuttings. 20-25 cm. long shoots are put into the sand medium for rooting. They root within 2 weeks.

By this process female plants are obtained more in number. The plants grown from seeds produce male plants in great numbers. In other words, the sex ratio is very wide, males disappointingly exceeding the female. The pest and disease control is the same as in bitter gourd.

There is a closely related species (M. *Cochin chinensis*) which bears very large fruit having the shape and size of a duck egg. It is grown in Assam, Bangladesh, South India, Andamans and the northern parts of West Bengal. Now its cultivation is spreading to the southern and western parts. In Philippines the tender twigs are used as pot herbs.

## KUNDRI (*Cephalandra indica*)

### Family : Cucurbitaceae

**Other name: Ivy gourd**

*Kundri* is a summer vegetable which is popular for its cooling effect. Hence it is preferred most in summer and the rains, Finger like green fruits are tender when used as vegetable. The vegetable clone is an improved and selected variety of the wild species of *Cephalandra indica* that bears more thick and oblong fruits of bitter taste. The wild species bear both male and female flowers in a plant. It is most interesting the vegetable clone bears only female flowers. Therefore no fertilization takes place due to the want of pollen. This is the reason why it produces the unfertilized seeds that do not contain umbryo and as such propagation by seed is not possible.

One-year old thick cuttings of the vine is planted in pits from November-December. The 1.5m long stem cutting is twined to form a ring of 20-30 cm in diameter and planted as in parwal. The vine ring should be treated with a fungicide before planting. Dithane M-45 can be used for this purpose. The soil of the pit should be maintained in a moist condition until the shoots sprout from the nodes of the vine ring. The normal irrigation should be given as needed.

*Kundri* is a heavy climber that needs support of a pergola or trellis for climbing and spreading. It is a perennial plant that yield for 5-8 years. Top dressing is applied round the plant within a diameter of 1 m. The stem is pruned to half of its length. To do this remove the thin vines first. Then reduce the stem to the half. Top dressing and regular irrigation are applied from the first week of February.

There are a good number of varieties which bear fruits of different shapes and sizes. But the varieties are not identified by names.

## RIBBED GOURD (*Laffa acutangula*)

### Family : *Cucurbitaceae*

**Other names : Hindi - Kali tori, Jhinga tori; Beng.-Jhiga, Tori ; Guj.-Ghisoda; Tel.-Birakaya; Tam.-Pirkankai.**

Ribbed gourd is very popular in the eastern and the southern parts of the country. It, like *Luffa cylindrica*, is rich in calcium, phosphorous and vitamin C. The water content is very high in these vegetables. They are summer and rainy-season crops. For the *rabi* crop sow seed in October to January and April-May for the *Kharif*. For raising seedlings in winter sow germinated seeds.

Sow 5-6 seeds per pit which are made 1.0-1.5 m. apart. Two selected seedlings are retained per pit. For top dressing nitrogen should be used less or the vegetative growth will increase at the cost of fruiting. In summer the vines trail over the ground but in the rains the support should be provided to spread the vines. But the long -fruited varieties always need trellis or pergola for the good shape of the fruits.

The fruits can be 15-75 cm. long according to the variety. In hot and dry summer some fruits may taste bitter. Then they are rejected. As a vegetable it should be tender and succulent. A sort of strong sponge grows on ageing.

**Varieties:** `Pusa Nasdhar', `Satputia', `Pilibhit', `Pusa Bikani', `Yard Long', `Coimbatore-I', `Dilip Pasand' etc.

## SPONGE GOURD (*Luffa cylindrica*)

### Family : Cucurbitaceae

**Other names: Hindi-*Ghiya tori, Nenua*; Beng.-*Dhundal*; Guj-*Turia*; Tel.-*Guthibira*; Mal.-*Kattu-peechal*.**

In gardens it may grow like weeds. A heavy creeper that covers a large space in no time. The vines of a single plant can cover a large tree top within a month or so. The fruits are large weighing 250-350g each. After picking in handling the skin gets spotted and looks unsightly that hardly can attract the customers. The sponge of the ripe fruits is used in making soles of the children shoes. Oil extracted from the seeds has its use in certain industries. In Bihar it is one of the popular vegetables. The fruits of the plants that grow wild can also be used as vegetable. They bear fruits just after the rains. But the garden varieties bear more.

Two seedlings per pit which is at a distance of 2 m. each way are retained. The cultural technique is the same as for ribbed gourd.

**Varieties:** `Pusa Chikni', `Bihar Best, etc.

## ASH GOURD (*Benincasa hispida*)

### Family : Cucurbitaceae

**Other names : Hindi-*Petha*; Beng.-*Chal Kumra*; Guj.-*Bhuru Kohlu*; Mar.-*Kohala*; Tel.-*Budidagummadi*; Mal.-*Kumbalangi*.**

Though it contains less vitamin the minerals like calcium and iron are enough. The tender fruits are light green in colour and covered with fine hairs. In this condition the fruit is used as vegetable. The mature or ripe fruits are covered with a ash-like white powdery substance. Hence the name `Ash gourd'. The mature fruits are used for preserves that have a great demand in confectionary. Ash gour is the largest of all gourds. A fruit may weigh 30-40 kg. But the fruits of the vegetable quality (at their tender stage) do not exceed 2 kg each.

Its culture is similar to that of pumpkin. It, unlike, pumpkin does not send out roots from the nodes when the vines spread over the land. Therefore the top dressing should be applied in the pits. It has only two varieties - one has the oval fruit and the other cylindrical.

## SNAKE GOURD (*Trichosanthes anguina*)

### Family : Cucurtitaceae

**Other names : Hindi-*Chachinda*; Beng.-*Chichinga*; Guj.-*Padavali*; Mar.-*Padwal*; Tam.-*Pudal*; Oriya-*Chhachhindara*; Bombay-*Chilonda*; Tel-*Lingapotla*.**

The fruits are long and striped that look like a snake. Hence the name. It is a vegetable of summer and the rains. It contains sodium, potassium, magnesium, calcium, phosphorous and vitamin A and C.

Snake gourd is a very quick growing plant. It can be grown easily. Two seedlings per pit are retained and allowed to grow. The pits are made 2m apart in rows. The vines need support for spreading. The fruits should grow straight. To make them perfectly straight a weight of 30-50 g is tied with the tail of the growing fruit with a soft string. The string obtained from a dry banana leaf is very suitable for this purpose. According to the variety a fruit may grow to a length of 30-110 cm. Snake gourd yields nearly 30 quintal per acre.

**Varieties:** `Co-1', `T.A.-19' etc.

## WATER MELON (*Citrullus vulgaris*)

### Family : Cucurbitaceae

**Other Names: Urdu, Hindi, Beng. And Mar – Tarbuj, Tarbur, Tarmui**

Water melon is a vegetable when green. But in the ripe stage a refreshing fruit. Sow 4-5 seeds per pit in October and November. If sown in December the germinated seeds should be used. The plant does not grow well in a cold weather. It assumes the normal growth when the temperature begins to rise in February. Since then you should apply top dressing and regular irrigation. The cultural technique is like that of cucumber. To prevent bacterial diseases the plants should be sprayed with Streptocyclin.

**Varieties:** `Sugar Baby', `Arkamanik', `Madhumilan', `Hybrid-4', `Hybrid-5', `Super sweet', `Jaunpuri' `Pusa Sarbati', Arkajyoti, `Asahi Yamato', `Charleston Grey', `Pusa Bedana' (Seedless), `Tetra-2', etc.

## MUSK MELON (*Cucumis melo*)

### Family : Cucurbitaceae

**Other names : Sans.-*Kharbuja*, `*Madhupaka*', Hindi, Punjabi, Guj. & Mar.-*Kharbuja*, Beng-*Kharmuj* Tam.-*Mulampazham*.**

The plants are grown from seeds which are sown after the rains. The ripe fruits are available in the market from winter to late summer. In its green stage it is a good vegetable with the cooling effect. Muskmelon is grown widely in Madhya Pradesh, Rajasthan, Punjab, Maharastra and Uttar Pradesh. The most varieties have a net like art work on the skin of the fruit. The colour of the ripe fruits are yellow or brown. There are few varieties which have smooth skin with 6-8 green stripes like the longitudes of the globe.

When the fruits are plucked in the green stage The bearing becomes more. Its culture is the same as cucumber.

**Varieties:** `Punjab Hybrid' ($F_1$), `Haramadhu', `Haragda', `Lucknow Safeda', `Kanpuria', `Mathuria', `Kabri', Jaunpuri, Motia, Chiranji',

`Jalgoon', `Mahaban', `Sankhda', Pusa Sarbati', Durgapur', Madhu, `Arkajeet', `Arka Rajhans', etc.

## PHUTI (*Cucumis melo* var. *momordica*)

### Family : Cucurbitaceae

**Other names : Hindi-*Phuti*; Beng. *Phuti*, Tel. *Peddakai*.**

*Phuti* in the green stage is a good vegetable like bottle gourd. The ripe fruit is fine with strong appetizing flavour. The fruit bursts on ripening. The peel is cream white and the Kernel is golden colour. There is an oval-shaped variety which grows throughout the year. Seeds of this variety are sown in October and June. Their fruits ripen in summer and automn respectively. *Phuti* is closely related to *Kharmuja* (Musk melon). The cultural method is the same as cucumber and water melon.

## SNAKE CUCUMBER (*Cucumis melo* var. *utilissimus*)

### Family : Cucurbitaceae

**Other names : Sans-*Bahukanda*; Hindi-*Kakri*; Tam- *Kakdi*; Beng.-*Kakur*.**

The tender fruits are like cucumber and eaten fresh and also cooked for a delicious curry. Fruits are green or greenish white and cylindrical. The fruits of the white variety have curvatures and warty skin.

Kakri, unlike *phuti*, is grown once a year. Seeds are sown in October. The cultural methods are the same as for cucumber.

There are many varieties of *Kakri* but they have not been identified with varietal names.

# *Fruit Vegetables*

Some fruit vegetables grown mostly from biennial or perennial plants are put in this group. They are propagated by seeds or cuttings. In some species ripe fruits are also used as vegetable, e.g. tomato, chilli, capsicum etc. In others they are as good as a quality fruit, e.g. papaya, banana, fig. etc.

## TOMATO (*Lycopersicon esculentum*)

### Family : Solanaceae

**Other names : Hindi-Tamatar; Beng.-Tomato, Belati Begun; Mar-Vel vangi; Guj.-Vilayithi vengan; Tam.-Takkali**

Tomato growing is very interesting. If virus infection and wilting are prevented the tomato growing is a fun. It requires less fertilizer and irrigation. Previously it was a winter crop but now there are many varieties which can be grown successfully as a *Kharif* crop. Besides the winter varieties planted in late winter yield fruits all through the summer. For raising early crops on the eve of winter the seedlings should be transplanted in the first week of September.

Tomato can be grown successfully in all sorts of soil type, i.e. sandy soil to heavy loam. For the heavy and quality production tomato needs quality potash fertilizer. It prefers potassium sulphate to potassium chloride. As potassium sulphate is not easily available as a fertilizer muriate of potash or wood ash is used instead. Because tobacco, like tomato, needs it for a quality production. As tobacco is an excellent exchange earner for India the total quality of imported potassium sulphate is utilized for growing tobacco. Hence unavailable for vegetable growing. Ash obtained from burning tobacco stems contains a good form of potash that can be used for growing quality tomato.

**Fig. 12:** A bunch of tomatoes.

For an acre of land 100g of seed is required. The congested seedlings in the seed bed may be destroyed by the damping off disease. 2-3 week old seedlings are transplanted 75-90 cm. apart on the ridges. The gap between the two adjacent ridges should be 60-75 cm. The total requirement of 30 kg.N per acre should be used in three equal split doses. No top dressing should be applied until the fruit setting takes place. Because more nitrogen and at the same time less potash causes more vegetative growth at the cost of flowering and fruiting. The following ingredients can be used in the fertilizer mixture for top dressing for an acre of cultivation.

Ammonium sulphate ............................... 10 kg.

Sulphate of potash .................................. 10 kg.

Magnesium sulphate ............................... 5 kg.

To remove the deficiency of the micronutrients foliar feed should be sprayed twice at a month interval. To prevent flower dropping Planofix should be sprayed on the plant as usual.

The stems are weak that need supports for growing erect. The fruits touching the damp ground from the trailing stems may be damaged by disease infection. To prevent fruit rotting fungicides like Dithane M-45, Bavistin, Blue copper should be applied by spraying alternately at an weekly interval. To prevent bacterial diseases spray Streptocyclin mixed with a little copper sulphate or Aurofungin sol.

**Varieties:** `Pusa Ruby', `Pusa Early Dwarf', `Sioux', `Marglobe', `Best of All', `S1.120', `Rama', `T-1', `Kalyanpur' `Angurlata', `Ponderose' `Keekruth', `Keekruth Ageti', `Tropical', `S1-12', `H.S.-101', `Hisar Lalit', `Money Maker', `La Bonita', `Krishnanagar-20', `Sutton Red Gem' etc.

## BRINJAL (*Solanum melongena*)

### Family : Solanaceae

**Other names : Hindi- *Baigan*; Beng. *Bagun, Bartaku*; Guj. *-Ringni*; Tam.- *Kathirikai*; Oriya- *Baigun*; Assam-*Jati Bengani*.**

Brinjal is a very common vegetable which is available through all seasons with the greater quantity in winter. The selected varieties are grown in summer and the rains. But there are innumberable varieties for winter cropping. Once planted the field can yield for two years. But in practice the field is planted once in every year. In other words the crop is not harvested for more than six months from a field.

There is hardly any other vegetable that has so many varieties as in brinjal. The innumerable shapes, sizes and colours of the fruits substantiate the statement. The shapes range from round, oval, oblong to long cylindrical. A wide variety of sizes from a very small duck egg size to a papaya size weighing up to 1 kg. are seen in brinjal. In the colour range the black, red, brown and purple predominate. The innumerable shades of these colours are abundant in brinjal.

Brinjal is a soft vegetable with taste and richness in nutrition. Brinjal, like tomato, is grown easily. But the borer insects cause a menace to the crop. If they are prevented it will fetch a good amount to the grower.

For the *rabi* crop the seedlings are planted in October-December and for the *kharif* it is done in April-June. 200g of seed is required for an acre of land.

Seed germinates within a week and 6 week-old seedlings are transplanted 60-80 cm. apart. The gap between the adjacent rows should be 1 m.

The top dressing is applied first on flowering and repeated at an interval of 6-7 weeks. A mixture of 15 kg. of urea and 5 kg. of muriate of potash may be used as top dressing. The average yield should be 2 kg. per plant that makes a production of one tonne per acre. Now hormone, foliar feed and biostimulants are being used to increase the production.

To check the shoot borer apply systemic granular insecticide like Furadan or Thimate at the rate of 3-5g per plant. It should not be used after fruit setting. Because the poisonous active principle will poison the vegetable.

**Varieties:** `Pusa Purple Long', `Pusa Purple Round', `Pusa Purple Cluster', `Pusa kranti', `T-1', to T-4', `Benaras Giant', `Black Beauty', `Muktakeshi', `S T-1', `ST-2', `P-8', `P-34', `Surti Gota', Manjri Gota', `Pusa Samrat', `Ajad Kranti', `Krishnanagar Purple Round' `Lurki', `Punjab Neelam', `Jamuni Gola' etc.

## CHILLI (*Capsicum frutescens*)

### Family : Solanaceae

**Other names : Hindi-*Lalmirch* ; Beng.-*Lanka*; Tel.-*Mirapa*; Tam.-*Milagay*; Kan.-*Mensina*; Mal.-*Mulaku*.**

Chilli serves both the purposes of vegetable and spice. It contains plenty of vitamin A,B and C along with phosphorous, potassium and protein. 100g of green chilli contains as much as 3 mg of vitamin C.

Chilli is a native of south America. It was first introduced in India from there and then it spreads to other countries. The shapes and sizes of chilli are innumerable. Green chillies are green, off-white or black in colour and then turn red, orange, yellow or blakish when ripe.

Excepting very cold weather chilli has a range of climatic tolerances. As a *kharif* crop it does not like heavy soils. But in *rabi* it prefers heavy soil that demand less irrigation. For a *Kharif* crop in heavy soil the land must have a good slope to drain off surplus water readily. The seedlings should be planted on the ridge of 30 cm. high.

The seed rate being 200g per acre. 6-8 week old seedlings are transplanted 40-50 cm. apart. The same gap should be in between the rows.

The first top dressing should be applied after 2 months of planting. It should contain 15 kg. of urea and 5 kg. of muriate of potash for an acre of land.

Aphids, thrips, mites and and mealy bugs attack the crop. To prevent flower drop spray Planofix (2m/1) twice at an interval of 10 days.

**Varieties:** `NP46A', `G-1', `G-2', and `G-3', `Jwala' `Suryamukhi', `P-41', `Patnai', `X-235', `Katki', `Dhani' (like a grain of rice)', `Nawabganji', `Manikchak', `Gole', `Bhutia' etc.

## CAPSICUM (*Capsicum annum*)

### Family : Solanaceae

**Other names : Hindi-*Simla mirch*; Beng.-*Misti-lanka*.**

Capsicum is highly nutritious, that contains Vitamin C in plenty. It is highly prized in the developed countries.

In the plains it is grown in winter. The seedlings planted in October-November bears fruits in December-January. The fruits are large, the length and breadth being equal. The plants grown in winter bear fruits upto May.

The seedlings are transplanted 45-60 cm. apart. The gap between the rows is also 60cm. The cultural method is almost the same as that of chilli.

**Varieties:** `California Wonder', `Yellow wonder', `Bullnose', `Bharat', `Vinidel', `Early Bounty', `Sutton gram Giant', `Sweet Pass', `Hungerian Wax' etc.

## PAPAYA (*Carica papaya*)

### Family : Caricaceae

**Other names : Hindi-*Papeeta*; Beng.-*Pape* ; Mar.-*Papaya*; Guj.-*Papayi*; Tam.-*Pappali*; Kan.-*Parangi-Mara*.**

Papaya is very popular and well-known vegetable and fruit. Its green fruits are used as vegetable while the ripe is a delicious fruit. Vegetable papaya contains vitamin A and papain. Papain help digest protein.

The soil having good drainage is essential for papaya. The seedlings are raised in the seed bed in April-May and transplanted in pits in June. The seeds should be treated with fungicide before sowing. The seedlings cannot stand water logging. If there is rain transplant the seedlings on a convex mound of the earth made on the pit already prepared. The large seedlings of 2-3 month old can also be transplanted. This is done after their sex identification. Because the female plants are in great demand as they bear fruit. Generally, seeds are sown on the pile of compost or cow manure in May. On the manure heap the seedlings grow very fast and flower within 60-80 days. The selected seedlings are lifted and made bare-root. All the leaves (leaving the growing ones) are cut leaving the leaf stalks. Wash the roots to remove the compost particles. Then dip the base of the seedlings in a bucket of water mixed with fungicide (3g/L) for 5 minutes. After this treatment keep them in shade for an hour. Then transplant them as usual in the pits.

Some prefers to sow seeds directly in the pit in the first week of June. 2-3 seedlings per pit is allowed to grow, only one of them which is female is selected and retained eventually. Obviously the selection can be made on flowering.

In a well-manured pit with plenty of nitrogen papaya seedlings grow very fast. Within 60 days they grow to a height of 60 cm. and show flower buds. The female bud is thick. Because it encloses a thick ovary which on fertilization developes into a fruit.

For pollination few male plants are grown in a field. 3-5 per cent of male plants in a field are enough for supplying pollen.

Papaya is a gross feeder. The food supplements should be applied at an interval of two months in the form of top dressing. In the kitchen garden, however, liquid manure is applied to feed papaya. The following ingredients can be mixed to prepare fertilizer mix for top dressing for an acre of papaya cultivation.

Urea........................................................ 25 kg.
Muriate of potash.................................... 5 kg.
Magnesium sulphate ............................... 2 kg.

From November to May 7-10 irrigations are needed. The occasional showers however, save irrigation. Heavy fruiting tells upon the size of the fruits. Both the shortage of nourishment and space for fattening may be wanting. The thinning out of the fruits in the early stage is the answer. With proper care the seedlings raised in May bear fruits that start ripening right from November.

Wilting, leaf curling, foot rot are the important diseases that cause immense harm to papaya culture. Good drainage of the soil prevent wilting and foot rot. Leaf curling is a viral disease that has no remedial measure. But its spread can be prevented by destroying the infected plants.

**Varieties:** `Washington', `Honey Dew' (Madhubindu), `Coorg Honey Dew', `Singapore', `Ceylon', `CO-1' is an improved strain of the Ranchi type, which has been originated at Coimbatore. `Hollywood', `Coimbatore 2',3,4, `Pusa 1-15', `Panth 1', `Pusa Delicious', `Pusa Majestic', `Pusa Giant', `Pusa Dwarf' etc.

## VEGETABLE BANANA (*Musa sapientum*)

### Family : Musaceae

**Other Names: Sans.- Kadali, Rambha, Hindi – Kela; Tel. – Arati; Tam. – Vazhai; Kan.- Bale.**

This is a vegetable variety of banana. The plants are very hardy, i.e. not susceptible to common diseases of banana.

Vegetable banana can be grown easily. A plant sends out many suckers which are used for propagation. In a clump not more than 4 plants are allowed to grow. The extra plants in their early stage are dug out with roots and planted in the new field in the rains. At the time of planting no manure or fertilizer is generally applied. The top dressing with plenty of humus is applied only once in the rains. The second dose is due to be applied in February. 4-5 irrigations are needed from February to May. In home gardens banana clumps are hardly irrigated. For planting pits are dug out 3 m. apart in rows. The distance between the two rows being the same. Before applying top dressing hoeing and weeding should be done. The mixture of the following ingredients is used as top dressing in an acre of land.

Humus.......................................................... 40 tne/acre
Urea ........................................................... 30 kg.
Pulverized oil cake ....................................... 100 kg.
Bonemeal/Super phosphate ........................ 80 kg.
Muriate of Potash ........................................ 50 kg.

For the individual clump of the home garden the following mixture is recommended.

Humus.......................................................... 3 buckets (10 litre cap.)
Pulverized oil cake ....................................... 2 kg.
Urea ............................................................ 150 g.
Super phosphate .......................................... 500 g.
Muriate of Potash ........................................ 500 g.

The disease-free plants should be planted. The suckers should be treated with a fungicide like Dithane M-45.

## DRUMSTICK (*Moringa oleifera*)

### Family : Moringaceae

**Other names : Hindi-*Shajna* ; Beng.-*Sajina*; Guj.-*Midhosara-gavo*; Tel.-*Mulaga*; Tam.-*Murungai*; Santal-*Munga arak.***

Drumstick is a popular vegetable of spring. With the introduction of the off-season varieties now it is available through all the seasons. It contains enough vitamin A, C and minerals like iron and phosphorous.

Moringa is a perennial tree which is propagated by seed or stem cuttings. Seeds germinate within a week or so. The cuttings (1.5m) of thick branches are taken when the plant remains dormant in winter. The base of the cutting is inserted 30 cm. deep at a distance of 3m in all directions. The soil round the cuttings should be kept moist with light watering at an interval of 10 days. After 6-8 weeks the cuttings will root and sprout shoots. Moringa is a very quick-growing plant. Practically no fertilizer is applied even in a commercial culture. It needs annual pruning which is done just after harvesting the fruits. In this process the half of the height of the plant is removed. When the tree will grow large one plant after another is removed so that the spacing comes to 6 m. between the plants. It is usually needed after 3-4 years of planting.

For better cropping the land should be fertilized with phosphate and potash fertilizers. In July after hoeing and weeding apply 1 kg each of super phosphate and muriate of potash by broadcasting round the plant up to the extent corroesponding to the spread of the branch. If the vegetative growth is not satisfactory apply the following mixture.

Humus.................................................... 2-3 baskets

Urea........................................................ 500 g.

Pulverized oilcake .................................. 1 kg.

There is a species of moringa which is annual. It is grown from seeds in the rains. Top dressing is applied in winter. The Agricultural Research Station of Bhavanisagar (Pin 638 451) has undertaken the research work on annual moringa. The research station has originated a new variety that can yield 400 sticks in course of a period of 10 months.

**Varieties:** `Yalpanam' - It is a perennial variety introduced from SriLanka. It is grown in the coastal region of South India. The stick is 1m in length. `Kodikkal' - It is also grown in the south. Fruits are small but fleshy and tasty. `Moolanur' - Grown in the Konkon coast. Fruits are 30-45 cm. long.

## GREEN JACK (*Artocarpas heterophyllus*)

### Family : Moraceae

Other names : Sans. & Tel. - *Panasa*; Hindi-*Kathal* ; Beng.-*Kanthal*; Mar.-*Phanas*; Tam.-*Pilapalam*.

The jack fruits in their green stage are used as vegetable that contains vitamin A and C along with protein, carbohydrates and some minerals. The seeds of ripe fruits are also used as vegetable.

Jacks bear heavily if properly looked after. Due to heavy bearing the fruit size becomes small. So half of the crop are picked and sold as vegetable. The small fruited varieties are specially grown for vegetable. The quality of a good vegetable variety are the small size, good shape and green colour of the fruits. The green jacks are found to be of three colours -green, brown or greenish brown. The green fruits are in great demand in the market for vegetable.

Generally jacks are propagated by seed. But the seedlings hardly resemble their mother in all respects. For this reason the selected variety needs to be propagated by air layering, inarching or budding.

Fruit drop and fruit rot may cause a menace to jack culture. Feeding with balance fertilizer once a year and spraying fungicide can control the trouble. The following mixture can be used for feeding the plant in the rains. The amount is for a 10-15 year old plant.

| | |
|---|---|
| Humus | 8 baskets |
| Pulverized Oilcake | 4 kg. |
| Urea | 300 g |
| Muriate of Potash | 1 kg. |

After hoeing and weeding the fertilizer mix is applied by broadcasting. To control disease spray fungicides like Dithane M-45, Bavistin, Blue Copper alternately at an interval of one month from October - January.

## FIG (*Ficus carica*)

### Family : Moraceae

**Other names : Hindi-*Anjir*; Beng.-*Dumur*; Guj.-*Anjir*; Kan.-*Anjura*; Mal-*Sima-yatti*.**

Fig, like banian tree, grows in uncultivated soil or on the stack of rubbish. Its minute seeds are dispersed by wind. As a vegetable its fruits are very nutritive but not tasty. It contains vitamins, carbohydrates, protein and plenty of iron.

Fig grows wild and bears like a wild plant. The tender fruits are used as vegetable. It has also garden varieties which are grown for ripe fruits. They in their green stage can also be used as vegetable.

# *Root Vegetable*

Though temperate many root vegetables grow in our climate. Not only that they have occupied a significant place in our produce also. So they could be grown only as winter crops, but now with the introduction of many new competent varieties they are now available through all seasons. They are also grown extensively on the hills to meet the increasing demand of the plains.

Since the beginning to recent past radish was mainly a winter vegetable. But now heat-tolerant varieties have been introduced which are being successfully grown throughout the year.

## RADISH (*Raphanus sativus*)

### Family : Cruciferae

**Other names : Hindi, Mar.,Guj.-*Muli*; Beng.-*Mula*; Tel., Tam., Kan. & Mal.-*Mullangi*.**

Radish is a common and popular root vegetable. Its tender foliage is also used as a pot herb. Radish is a short term crop, i.e. can be raised within 45-60 days. It is not usually troubled by pests and diseases. Hence the popularity.

The soil should be prepared finely granular. The tilth of the land should be 25 cm. deep. The following mixture is used as the basal dressing for an acre of land.

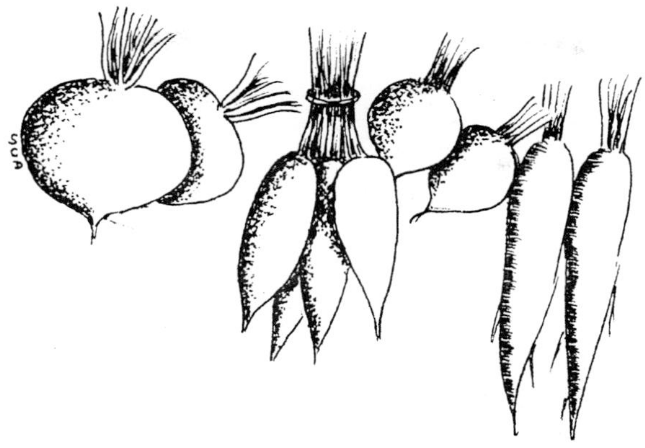

**Fig. 13:** Root vegetables (Turnip, Carrot, Beet and Radish)

Humus.................................................. 48-72 tne
Urea...................................................... 70 kg.
Super phosphate..................................... 40 kg.
Muriate of Potash.................................. 30 kg.

The seed rate being 3-5 - 4.5 kg. per acre. The seeds are sown in two ways. First by broadcasting uniformly in the entire plot and the second being sowing in rows on the ridges. At the six leaf stage the weak seedlings are removed. After two weeks again it may need thinning. The healthiest and vigorous ones are retained 20-30 cm apart for setting big size roots. Radish needs more irrigation which should be given at an interval of 7-12 days.

**Varieties:** `White Icicle', `Pusa Himani', `Rapid Red', `White Tipped', `Scarlet Globe', `French Breakfast', Japanese White', `Pusa Desi', `Pusa Chetaki', `Jaunpuri', `Bombay Red', `Contai Long', `Chinese White', `Kalyani White', `Kalimpong Red', `Pusa Reshmi' etc.

## CARROT (*Daucas sativa*)

### Family : Umbelifareae

**Other names : Sans.-*Shikha-mula*; Hindi-Beng., Guj. & Punjabi - *Gajar*, Mar.-*Gazara*; Kan-*Gajjari*.**

Carrot is very popular for its vitamin contents. Its name `Carrot' has come from the word `carrotine' which is synnonymous with vitamin. It is rich in vitamin A,B,C and minerals like potassium, phosphorous, iron and carbohydrates. Carrot and corriander belong to the same family. The leaves of carrot is also nutritious.

Rich heavy soil is ideal for growing carrot. Soil acidity should be at 6.5. The heavy soil needs more humus than the light soil. For an acre of carrot the following mixture is necessary as basal dressing.

Humus .................................................. 48-70 tne.
Urea ....................................................... 20 kg.
Super phosphate ...................................... 50 kg.
Muriate of Potash .................................... 60 kg.

For top dressing use the following mixture.

Urea ......................................................... 70 kg.
Pulverized oilcake ..................................... 50 kg.

Seed is sown from September to December in the plains. The seed requirement is 2 kg. per acre. Seed germinates within a week. Seed is sown directly in the field. Because the transplanted seedlings do not grow well. For facilitating hoeing and weeding the seedlings should be in rows while thinning out for spacing some should be dug out and the others will be allowed to grow to the standard size. The production of 70-80 quintals is obtained from an acre of land.

**Varieties:** `Half-long Nantes', `Coreless', `Chantaney' `Pusa Kesar', `Early Nantes', `Stream Lines' `Denvars' etc.

## BEET ROOT (*Beta vulgaris*)

### Family : Chenopodiaceae

**Other names : Hindi-Chukansar ; Beng.-Beet.**

Beat is a kind of spinach (*Palak*). But it does not set seed in the plains. There are two types of beet, e.g. one for vegetable and the other is sugar beet which is used in the sugar industry. Beet is grown exclusively in winter. No variety has been introduced to grow in summer and the rains. Therefore its increasing demand in the off season is met by the crop of the hills.

Carrot and beet are grown in the same type of soil but beet prefers slightly alkaline soils. In other words, $P^H$ 7 is suitable for growing beet. It grows well in a soil having enough organic manure. Therefore chemical fertilizer should be used with restraint. The major portion of nitrogen should be supplied through the use of oilcake.

Seed is sown on the ridges. Thinning out of the seedlings should be made to maintain a spacing of 20 cm. between the two seedlings. The gap between the rows should be 30 cm.

## TURNIP (*Brassica rapa*)

### Family: Brassicaceae

**Other names : Hindi-*Shaljum*; Beng.-*Shalgam*; Mar & Oriya-*Salgum*; Tel. & Kan.-*Turnip*.**

Turnip, like radish, is easy to grow. It becomes ready for picking within 6-8 weeks of sowing. The roots of turnip are round and flattish at the poles. It remains to be edible so long it is tender and crisp. When this stage is over it is fed to the cattle.

The agrotechnique is like that of radish. The yield per acre is 7.5-10 tonnes. In some states of the country turnip is very popular while in others it is scarcely grown. In the western countries it is very popular.

**Varieties:** `Purple Top', `White Globe', `Golden Ball' `Snow Ball', `Pusa Chandrima', `Pusa Kanchan', `Pusa Sweti'.

## PARSNIP (*Pastinaca sativa*)

### Family : Umbelliferae

Parsnip is closely related to carrot. But it is a rare vegetable in this country. It is a native of Mediterranean region. In India it is mainly grown in the kitchen garden.

The cultural method is almost the same as that of carrot. The viability of seed is only one year. Therefore fresh seed should be sown.

Seed takes few weeks to germinate, which should be sown on ridges at a distance of 30 cm. 2-3 week-old seedlings are thinned out to maintain a spacing of 10 cm. between the two.

**Variety:** `Yellow crown'.

**Fig. 14:** Parsnip.

# *Tuber Vegetable*

The tuberous-root vegetables are not considered green vegetable. They grow underground and after digging out the tubers can be stored for a year or so. Though grown once in a year the supply is perennial. Hence so popular.

## POTATO (*Solanum tuberosum*)

### Family: Solanaceae

**Other names : Hindi & Beng.-*Alu* ; Mar. & Guj. *Batata*; Tel.-*Bangala dumpa* ; Kan.-*Batale* ; Mal. *Krulam Kizhangu.***

Potato is considered one of the most nutritious, popular and economic crop of the most part of the world. India produces potato in large quantities. Still it is not at par with the European countries. Because the per capita consumption is 200 kg. per annum, whereas in India it is not more than 5 kg. Potato contains 20 per cent of carbohydrate and two per cent of protein along with plenty of minerals like calcium, magnesium, phosphorous, sulphur, iron and vitamin C. In the plains potato is grown in winter, whereas in the hills it is done in summer. It can be grown well in a temperature of 20°C. A slightly acid soil with $p^H$ 5.2 - 6.4 is suitable for potato.

That is why liming is not necessary in the soil for growing potato. Medium to heavy loam is ideal for its culture. A heavy soil however needs plenty of humus in the form of cowmanure, compost etc. to improve the soil structure suitable to potato. Heavy soil needs less irrigation. At the time of soil preparation if it is thoroughly dried the potato cultivation will be easy, and the crop will not need more than three irrigations. In the light soil the colour of the tubers becomes bright but its culture needs more irrigation. Besides the measure against termites and red ants has to be taken. Potato needs more potash for the quantity and quality of the tubers. The quality produce can be preserved well. So the crop should be fed with plenty of potash. The quantity of seed potato required is very high which often becomes a limiting factor. The small size tubers (2-3 cm. diameter) are used as seed potato. They are available in the market in the planting season in the sprouted condition. If the size of the seed potato becomes large the seed rate will rise to 8-10 quantals per acre. The large sprouted tubers are however divided with a sharp knife so that each piece must have an eye with a sprout. Thus from a large tuber a number of divisions as seed can be obtained. The requirement of seed by tuber division is 2-3 quintals per acre.

**Fig. 15:** Pototo planted on the ridges.

To reduce the seed requirement a new type of seed named TPS (true potato seed) has been innovated. The process involves the raising of seed from potato fruit. Next season the seeds are sown in the nursery bed. Within two months the seedlings will produce very small tubers. They are dug out and stored for the next season. On sprouting they are used as seed. Such small seed tubers are known as `microtuber'.

The most of the diseases of potato are seed-borne. So the seed should be disease free. The spotted tubers or those having The mark of a ring within should never be used as seed. The supply of quality seed potato comes from Punjab and Manali. When the large tubers are used as seed they are collected and spread over dry floor of a dark room. In this condition within a few weeks almost all the eyes of the tuber will sprout shoots. Use a sharp knife treated with rectified spirit to divide the tubers. Each division weighing 10-20 g must have at least one sprout. Then they should be treated to remove the seed-borne diseases. Any of the following chemicals/fungicides can be used for this purpose.

Agallol-6, Eretan-6, Ceresan, Dithane-M 45.

Mix 150g of any of the above chemical in 100 litres of water. Deep the seed in the solution for 2-5 minutes. This quantity of the solution is sufficient for treating 2 quintals of potato seed. This will prevent late blight, ring, fusarium wilt etc. To prevent bacterial wilt and foot rot treat the seed with Agrimycin (6g/10L) or Plantomycin (10g/10L). For other disease use Bavistin (1 g/L) for treating the seed. The treated seed should be kept in baskets for few hours until the moist surface dries up.

Use the following ingredients while preparing the soil. The quantities mentioned are for an acre of land.

Humus.................................................... 48-72 tne
Urea........................................................ 70 kg.
Super phosphate...................................... 70 kg.
Muriate of Potash.................................. 50 kg.

The ridges are made 30 cm. apart. By Scooping soil seeds are planted 10-15 cm. deep and 30 cm. apart on the low ridges. They should be kept moist by sprinkling water with the help of a water can. When the shoots will grow 10-15 cm high the ridges will be made high by putting earth from the adjacent furrows. Just before the irrigation apply top dressing of 15kg. of urea or 100 kg. of ammonium sulphate per acre.

The irrigation is needed on the basis of the moisture content of the soil that is determined by moisture retentive capacity of a particular soil type. Generally 3-8 irrigations are required for a crop. When apical vegetative growth is stopped tubers begin to swell even when the stems start drying. The yield per acre may be 250 quintals at the highest.

**Disease:** The early and late blight may cause a menace to potato growing. The late blight causes brown spot on the leaves and stems. The spraying with Dithane M-45 can prevent the late blight. In a dry weather the disease cannot spread. On the contrary the rise in humidity in the atmosphere causes the trouble. The use of seed treated with Dithane-M 45 can prevent the disease. Prevention is the most important because there is no cure for the disease. Once a crop is infected the land should not be used for growing potato for 3-4 years.

The insects like termites, ants, mole crickets, leaf-cutting beetles may cause harm to the crop. To prevent them use 15 kg. of Aldrin or BHC 10% per acre while preparing soil.

**Varieties:** `Kufri Chandramukhi', `Kufri Alankar', `Kufri Chamatkar', `Kufri Jyoti', `Kufri Jiban', `Royal Kidney', `Kufri Bahar', `Kufri Moti', `Kufri Loukar', `C-1', `F-5134' etc.

## SWEET POTATO (*Ipomoea batatas*)

### Family : Convalvulaceae

**Other names : Hindi-*Mitha alu, Sakarkand*; Beng.-*Lal alu, Ranga alu*; Mar.-*Ratalu*; Guj.-*Kanangi*; Tel.-*Chelagada*; Kan.-`*Genasu'*; Oriya `*Kanda'*.**

Sweet potato is a carbohydrate - rich vegetable. It is very popular for its sweetness. It has a white variety which is known as `Sakarkand Alu' in Hindi. The tubers of this variety are coloured with a red pigment for fetching the same price as the red type. Both the varieties are grown in the same process. Sandy loam is highly suitable for sweet potato. Both for *rabi* and *kharif* crops sweet potato is grown. The planting material are the vine cuttings which are planted in the cutting bed for rooting. A bed of moist soil in shade is suitable for rooting. The long vines are cut to pieces of 30 cm. long for rooting prior to planting in the field. The sprouted tubers can also be planted. The gap between the plant to plant and row to row should be 60 cm. And for such planting 8-10 thousand cuttings are required.

Apply following fertilizer ingredients as basal dressing.

Humus........................................................ 50-70 tne/acre
Urea .......................................................... 20 kg.
Super phosphate ........................................ 40 kg.
Muriate of potash/wood ash ....................... 30 kg.

The cuttings should be planted in rows. After a month the rows should be raised by earthing. Just before the operation apply top dressing of 40 kg. of urea per acre that should be followed by irrigation. For the *rabi* crop irrigate the field at an interval of 10-15 days. In the light soil when the tubers develop the layer of soil over them is found to split up. Dig out the tubers when the vines dry up. The yield per acre varies from 200-250 quintals.

## YAM (*Dioscorea* spp.)

### Family : Dioscoreaceae

**Other names : Sans.-*Pindalu*; Hindi & Beng.-*Chupri alu, Khamalu*; Tel.-*Pendalamu*; Kan.-*Onthalaigasu*; Assam-*Katalu*; Bombay-*Goradu.***

Yam is rich in carbohydrates. It has a number of species, some of them have spines on the stem. Generally the species *Dioscorea alata* is cultivated as vegetable. It has few varieties most of them have cylindrical roots that become thick and go downwards. There are also few that have dilated roots. On the basis of the shape and size of the roots 75 cultivars have been identified in this country. In the third volume (Page 72) of Wealth of India there is an illustration of 75 cultivars or species. Yam contains an alkaloid named `diosgenin' which is used to prepare contraceptives.

The vines develop a sort of outgrowth, the botanical term of which being `bulbil'. It is used to propagate the plant. It sprouts shoots like the swollen roots. Generally the roots sprout shoots from the crown. The new sprouts with at least 250g of the flesh is planted in pits 1.5-3m. apart. A plant produces 25-75 bulbils in a season. They are not however, produced from flowers. The large plant, in light soil produces plenty of seeds. A plant in a well manured pit can produce a huge root weighing as much as 40 kg. in course of 8-10 months.

The tubers are planted from April-July. In April-May and November-December yam needs irrigation. The roots swell rapidly in the period from October - January. In this period the soil should not run dry.

A pit well fertilized with phosphate and potash is suitable for growing yam. The last dose of nitrogen should be applied in August. In kitchen gardens stakes are provided so that the vines can climb up and spread. In the field, however, the trailing vines spread over the ground. In this process the root hardly exceeds 2 kg. per pit. For this reason the pit are made 1.5m apart in the field. Thus an acre of land accomodates 2000 plants. The yield varies from 2 to 4 tonnes. The roots are harvested from October to March.

## ELEPHANT FOOT (*Amorphophallus campanulatus*)

### Family : Araceae

Other names : Sans.-*Arsaghna*, Hindi,-*Zamin-Kand*, Beng.-*O1*, Guj & Mar.-*Suran*, Tel.-*Kanda*, Mal.-*Chena*.

Elephant foot is grown in all parts of the country. It prefers the moist climate for its vegetative growth and dry weather for the growth of its corm. In the cold weather the corm remains dormant. In summer the shoots sprout from the dormant corm. So its subterranean part (corm) is perinnial and the aerial part (shoot) is annual. The plant with its foliage looks like an umberella, i.e. an uniformly spreading head on a 100 cm. high green stem. The green stem and the leaf salks are used as a pot herb. In certain variety the corm and stem have some acridity due to the presence of calcium oxalate. The improved varieties are also free from the chemical (Calcium oxalate). The wild varieties develop the chemical in plenty. Hence inedible. Elephant foot is rich in vitamin A and B, minerals and carbohydrates.

Elephant foot can be grown successfully in light, medium and heavy soils. The soil containing one-thirds of humus yields more. In early summer the shoot is sprouted from the crown of the corm. But if the corm is divided into pieces with the flesh of 300-400g each a number of planting materials can be obtained from a large corm. Each division must have its share of the skin. Because the shoots sprout from the skin of the corm that should be divided in March. After a month the shoots will begin to sprout from the corm divisions, and it is then they are ready for planting.

Elephant foot is planted in pits 60cm apart. Apply 2 tea-spoonful of Plantomycin or Pusamycin in each pit to prevent foot rot and wilting. After division the pieces of the corm are put in the nursery bed in shade. They are covered with half decomposed straw and a medium level of moisture is maintained by sprinking water that helps sprout shoots early.

For an acre of land 4-5 quintal seed corm is required. The well-sprouted corm pieces from the nursery bed is planted one in each pit. Before starting the monsoon rains in June irrigation is needed twice a month. If water for irrigation is wanting the planting should be delayed until June. After a month of planting the rows of pits are raised by earthing thus making ridges and furrows as usual. After 3 months of planting top dressing is applied with 75-100 kg. of urea per acre. Again after six weeks the second top dressing is applied with the same material and at the same rate. To prevent the disease incidence fungicides like Bavistin, Dithane-M 45 and Blue copper are sprayed alternately at a month's interval. The corm will be dug out when the plant will decline. The crop yield varies from 50-100 quintals per acre. In kitchen gardens one corm is allowed to grow for 2-3 years. The corm puts forth shoot every year in May-June. This practice is common as the plant is not well looked after with proper feeding just contrary to the commercial culture.

**Varieties:** `Kouvur' (*Gajendra*), `Santragachi', `Bombai' etc.

## GIANT TARO (*Colocasia gigentea*)

### Family : Araceae

**Other names : Sans.-Kachu, Hindi-Arvi; Beng.-Mankachu, Oriya-Saru.**

This species is larger than any other taro in cultivation. Hence the name. The cylindrical root continues to grow above the ground like a stem. It takes 2-3 years to grow to a length of 1 m. and the root of this size is harvested. The girth of the root varies from 15-20 cm. in diameter. One standard root weighs 15-20 kg. The portion close to the growing point is more tender and delicious. The vegetable is rich in carbohydrates and minerals.

For propagation, the stem-like root is divided into pieces each having 5-10 cm. length. The stem is cut crosswise and planted horizontally. Like elephant foot, the cut pieces are put on the nursery bed for sprouting. The sprouted root divisions are planted one in each pit lying 1.5 m. apart in June. It is a moisture loving plant. So for better production irrigate the field from November to May, once in a month. Top dressing is applied once in the rains. Taro needs more potash for its better growth.

Taro, like elephant foot, may develop calcium oxalate which is the cause of acridity. The improved cultural technique with goog feeding and irrigation is sure to yield roots of good quality.

## TARO *(Colocasia esculenta)*

### Family : Araceae

**Other names: Sans.-*Kachu*, Hindi-*Arvi*, Beng.-*Mukhi kachu*,Mar.-*Alu*, Kan.-*kachchi*, Mal.-*Shembu*.**

Taro is a common root vegetable rich in carbohydrates and minerals. The corm-like roots grow round the base of the plant. The base itself is the bigger corm. A number of round or oval cormels grow from it which are used as vegetable.

Both the corm and cormels are used for propagation. But the plants grown from the corms yield more. The roots are dug out from September to November. The cormels are sent to the market as vegetable and the corms are stored until they sprout. For raising the early crop they are planted in March-April.

The soil preparation is like that of potato. The sprouted corm or cormels are planted in rows 30 cm apart. The gap between the two adjacent rows being 45 cm. After a month the top dressing is applied on the rows which are then raised by earthing thus making ridges and furrows as usual. The summer, planting needs frequent irrigation usually at an interval of 2 weeks. The roots are dug out in June-July when the vegetable fetches a good price.

To save irrigation and at the same time to make the produce cheap taro is planted in June and the root is dug out in October. For planting an acre of land 2-3 tonnes of seed corm is required. The yield varies from 10-15 tonnes.

Varieties: Common taro and tetraploid taro. The later being very large in size.

## EDDOE (*Colocasia* sp.)

### Family : Araceae

Other names : Hindi- *Panikachu*, Beng.- *Jal kachu*, Oriya- *Saru*.

The plant is tall resembling taro. It grows in submerged land like a bog plant. In land it grows like a common taro. But in water it grows to a height of 2m. Its root is stem like with close similarity with that of giant taro. The entire plant, i.e. from the swollen root to the leaf is used as vegetable with the preference of large and thick leaf stalks. The plant sends out plenty of runners, which are slender, long (rope-like), and tender. They are also used as vegetable.

Suckers or runners propagate the plant. For having planting materials the plant are grown in the garden under the shade of a tree where a plant sends out plenty of suckers if the soil is kept moist. Besides if planted along the side of the irrigation channel of the field the plantlets will grow in plenty. Along the water line of a pond they also planted for multiplication.

Eddoe is grown in marshes and shallow ponds. In summer when they become nearly dry mix the following mixture to the mud of 1 sq.m. evenly.

Humus........................................................ 2 buckets (10 litre cap.)
Pulverized oilcake ....................................... 250g.
Urea ........................................................... 100 g
Super phosphate ......................................... 150 g
Muriate of potash ........................................ 150 g

The suckers should be planted after 2-3 weeks of manuring. After planting release water to be a depth of 5-7 cm. As the plants grow more water will be required. Generally it is accumulated due to the occasional norwester or pre-monsoon showers. In the rains more water accumulates and the depth of water should not raise more than 60 cm. It grows well in water of 30 cm. deep. The vegetable becomes ready after 4 months of planting.

## JERUSALEM ARTICHOKE (*Helianthus tuberosum*)

### Family : Compositae

**Other names: Hindi- *Hatichuk*, Beng.- *Brahmokha*, Punjab- *Hathipich*.**

The flower head of globe artichoke is used as vegetable, but Jerusalem artichoke is a root crop, which contains insulin. Hence useful to diabetic patient. The plant is tall and slender; the leaves are wide and thick. The large corms are used as vegetable and cormels are used as planting materials. It is grown as *rabi* or *kharif* crop. For a *rabi* crop plant cormels in October-November and for the *kharif* it is done in April-May. For an acre of planting nearly 80 kg.of seed corm is needed.

The planting and after care is like that of potato. Plant the cormels 45 cm. apart and 8 cm. deep. The gap between the two adjacent rows being 90 cm. The seed corm should be treated with fungicide before planting.

# *Bulb Vegetable*

The plant of this group form bulbs at the base of the plant. The bulbs are used as both spice and vegetable. The foliage is used like leafy vegetable. Both seeds, bulbs and off shoots are used to propagate the plant. The plants are monocotyledonous and as such grow fibrous roots. The mature bulbs are dug out and stored for a year or so.

## ONION (*Allium cepa*)

### Family : Liliaceae

Other names : Hindi-*Piyaz*; Beng.-*Pyanj*; Guj.-*Dungari*; Tel.-Nirulli; Mal.-*Chuvannaulli*.

Onion forms large round bulbs whereas shallot forms small spindle -shaped bulbs. Onion tends to form one large bulb per plant whereas shallot grows a clump of small bulbs. Shallot is more pungent than onion. Hence more a spice than a vegetable.

Onion is grown in all parts of India. Maharastra leads in onion production. Onion contains protein, carbohydrates, calcium, phosphorous, iron, vitamin A and C, and iodine.

Onion is mainly a winter crop. It grows well in 10-15°C. It is grown from seed. For an acre of cultivation 2 kg. of seed is required. Seed is sown in the seed bed and 6-7 week-old seedlings are pricked out and planted in the field. The following manure and fertilizer is used as basal dressing.

Humus........................................................ 50 tne/acre
Urea ......................................................... 50 kg.
Super phosphate ......................................... 40 kg.
Muriate of Potash ....................................... 70 kg.

The distance from plant to plant and row to row is the same, which is 15cm. only. Apply top dressing of 50 kg. of Urea after hoeing between the rows. Irrigate as necessary.

Onion needs more potash. In deficiency of which the tips of the folliage begin to dry up. The bulbs grow and mature within 120 days of planting. When the plants show the sign of decline irrigation should be stopped. Then the leaves will begin to dry up. It is then the bulbs will be dug out. An acre yields 6000-8000 kg. of bulbs.

To prevent disease spray fungicides at an interval of 4 weeks right from the seedling stage.

**Varieties:** `Pusa Red', `Ratnar', `Early Grano', `Red Patna', `Patna White', `Poona Red', `Nasik Red', `Nasik White', `Bellary Red' etc.

## SHALLOT (*Allium ascalonicum*)

### Family : Liliaceae

**Other names :** ***Hindi*- Gandana, *Beng.*- Gundhun.**

Shallot in common parlance is also called onion. Its characteristics have been discussed in the foregoing vegetable. It is used as a spice rather than a vegetable. Shallot, unlike onion, is propagated by the cloves of a bulb. Because its seed is not available. Its seed may be available in the country to which it is native. It has been introduced in this country. The cloves are small and spindle-shaped and grow in a clump. The cloves are separated and used as planting materials. The tips of the cloves are cut and planted as usual in rows like onion. After-care is the same as that of onion.

**Variety:** Not recognized in this country.

## GARLIC (*Allium sativum*)

### Family : Liliaceae

Other names : Sans.-*Arishtha*; Hindi & Guj.-*Lasan*; Beng. & Mar.-*Rasum*; Kan.-*Bellulli*; Punjab-*Thom*.

Garlic is however more a spice than a vegetable. It contains protein, carbohydrates, calcium, phosphorous, iron and vitamine B and C.

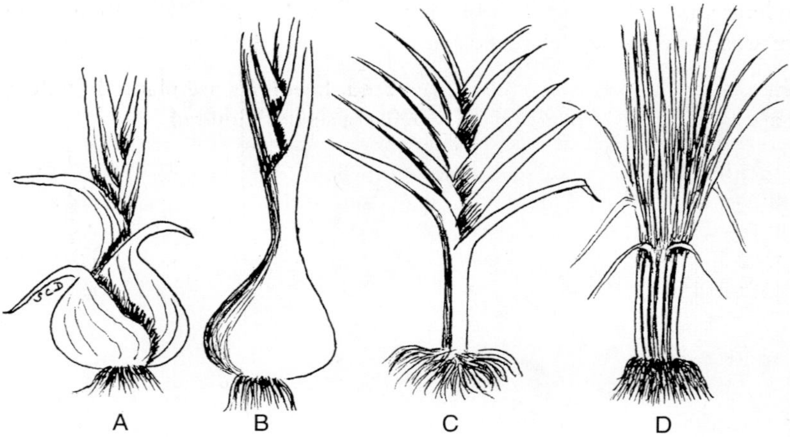


**Fig. 16:** Bulbous vegetables. A. Onion, B. Garlic, C. Leek, D. Ceboule

Each plant grows one bulb consisting of a good number of cloves covered with scales. The bulb is divided into cloves. Each clove is planted as a seed. An acre of planting needs one quintal of garlic bulb. The cloves are planted 10cm. apart in the beginning of winter. The growing technique is the same as that of onion.

The yield of garlic bulbs varies from 1.5-2 tonnes.

**Variety:** Not recognized in this Country.

## LEEK (*Allium porrum*)

### Family : Liliaceae

Leek is a vegetable of the temperate climates. In the plains it is grown mainly in kitchen garden in winter. Leek does not form conspicuous bulbs. The underground part is simply a bit thicker than the rest. The bulb and leaves are used as vegetable, salad and spice.

The plant, like onion, is grown from seed. Seedlings are planted 15-20 cm. apart. For an acre of planting 800-1000 g of seed is required.

When the plants grow large the row of plants should be earthed to cover the base of the plants, that helps blanch the basal part. The loss of chlorophyll make the stem-like base crips and tasty. Leek unlike onion, does not form a perfect bulb which cannot be stored for subsequent use. So it is like a green vegetable.

## CEBOULE (*Allium fistulosum*)

### Family : Liliaceae

**Other names :** ***Eng.-*** **Welsh onion;** ***Beng.- Pat Pyanj.***

Ceboule is like a sort of leek but slender and thin. It is grown from seeds and clump divisions. The plant, like shallot, grows a number of offshoots to form a clump. The whole plant leaving the fibrous roots is used as salad or pot herb.

The cultural method is like that of leek.

# *Malvaceous Vegetable*

## OKRA (*Abelmochus esculentus*)

### Family : Malvaceae

**Othernames : *Eng.*- Lady's Finger; *Hindi*- Bhindi; *Beng.*- Dheras; *Guj.*- Binda; *Tam.*- Vendai; *Kan.*- Bhende.**

Okra is very well-known and popular vegetable. It contains vitamin A, B and C in sufficient quantities. It is a vegetable of hot climate, But the plants grown in late winter give an early crop in spring. Okra can be grown successfully in light, medium or heavy soil. In heavy soils the plant grow tall. On the contrary a plant of light sandy soil becomes dwarf and bears early.

Seed is sown from January - July. The seed rate being 6-7 kg. per acre. Seeds are sown 30-35 cm. apart and 1 cm. deep on the ridges. The gap between the two rows should be 60 cm. Seed should be treated with fungicide before sowing.

The following ingredients are used in basal dressing in an acre of land.

Humus.......................................................... 48-70 tne
Urea ............................................................... 50 kg.

Super phosphate ........................................ 60 kg.
Muriate of Potash ....................................... 30 kg.

B A

**Fig. 17:** Malvaceous vegetable. A. Okra, B. Indian sorrel.

On flowering a top dressing with 60 kg. of urea is applied.

The tender fruits are edible. So the growing fruits must be checked every day if they have become ready for picking. The yield per acre is 6000 kg. The exhausted plant may cut back to the height of 30 cm. from the ground. The new shoots will grow, that will bear in their turn. The process is known as ratooning. A top dressing of urea of 30 kg. should be repeated.

Mosaic virus being the main trouble in the field of Okra. Now-a-days however virus resistant varieties have been originated. The stem and foot borer also give troubles.

**Varieties:** Lucknow Dwarf', `Long Green', `Velvet Green' `Smooth Velvet', `Long White', `Red Wonder', `Samalkota', `Pusa Sawani', `Pusa

Makhmali', P.B.-7', `Parvani Kranti', `Improved Sawani', `Coimbatore 1' etc.

## ROSELLE (*Hibiscus sabdariffa*)

### Family : Malvaceae

**Other names: *Hindi*- `Lal-ambari'; *Beng.*- Lal-mista', `Patwa', Chukar; *Mar.*- Lal-ambadi; *Assam*- Chukiar.**

The plant is closely related to the Deccan hemp (Hibiscus cannabinus). The plants grow like a shrub but not perennial. The fruits are small and entirely covered with thick sepals. The fruits are not edible. The sepals with sour taste is used as vegetable. The preserves like *chatny* and pickle are also prepared easily.

Reselle pickle which is very easy to prepare is very tasty. Separate the sepals and add 10 per cent of salt to the vegetable. After two days put it in the sun for a week. Then add spices according to the taste.

Roselle is annually grown in the kitchen garden. Once grown it grows like a weed from the next season.

# *Salad Vegetable*

## LETTUCE (*Lactuca sativa*)

### Family: Compositae

**Other names : *Hindi & Beng.*- Kahu Salad ; *Tel*- Kavu; Tam.-Salutti.**

Lettuce is a leafy vegetable which is used fresh as salad and in preparing *pokorda*. It is very nutritious, which is rich in protein, vitamine and minerals. Lettuce can be grown through all seasons. But in summer the plants bear flower early. In winter, however, it grows nicely. The plant with large leaves are very beautiful as such it can be grown with the ornamentals.

Seed germinate within a few days. But the germination retards in the temperature above 27°C. In light soil lettuce grows fast. For an acre of cultivation 1500g of seed is needed. Its cultural procedure is the same as recommended for cabbage.

The seedlings are transplanted 25-30 cm apart on ridges. It is usually grown in semi-shade of a kitchen garden. The scorching mid-day sun makes the leaves pale and stiff. On the contrary the leaves of the plants grown in semi-shade becomes bright and crisp. Those varieties which form head like cabbage is known as `head-type'.

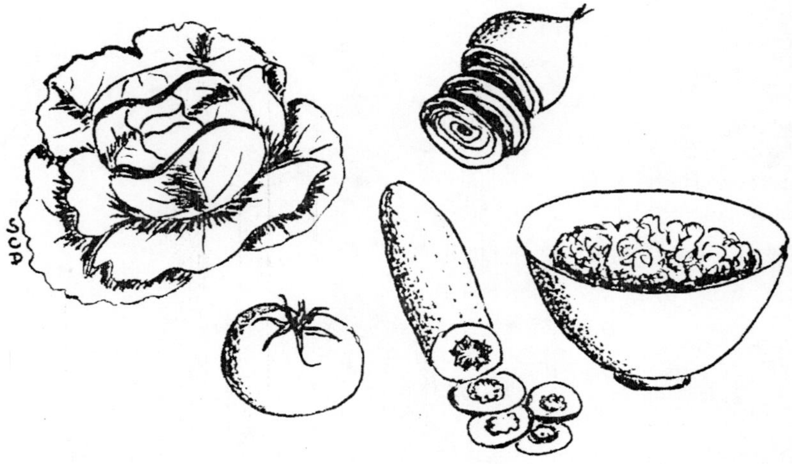

Fig. 18: Salad (Lettuce, Tomato, Cucumber and Onion)

Fig. 19: Lettuce

## CELERY (*Apium graveolens*)

### Family : Umbelliferae

Other names: *Hindi-* Shalari, Ajmud; *Beng.-* Randhuni; *S.India-*Ajmod or Ajmoda.

This vegetable is comparable to coriander. The leaves and leaf stalks are used as salad. The dry leaves in a powered form is used to add a spicy flavour to the cooked food. Its seed is considered a good spice in the cold countries. Celery contains protein, calcium, phosphorous, iron along with vitamin A and C.

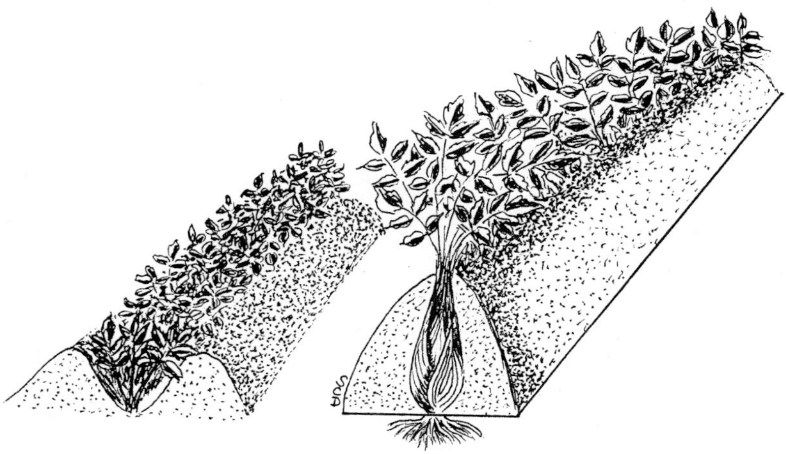

A B

**Fig. 20:** Celery. A. Planted in a furrow, B. A ridge is formed by earthing to cause blancing.

Seed is sown in seed pans. It takes 1-2 weeks to germinate. Seedlings are minute that need care. 6-8 week-old seedlings are transplanted 25-30 cm apart in rows. The seed rate for an acre of land being 1500 g. The fertilizer mixture given below is used as basal dressing.

Humus........................................................ 50-60 tne.

Urea ........................................................... 50 kg.

Super Phosphate ......................................... 40 kg.

Muriate of Potash ....................................... 50 kg.

At an interval of 3 weeks apply top dressing of 15 kg. of urea twice.

The basal portion of celery, like leek, should be made blanch by earthing. So make a furrow between the lines and lift the soil on the adjacent row to make a ridge of 40 cm. high. This can be done gradually by more than one operation. In this process the base of the plant covered by soil will lose chlorophyll thus making blanch and crips.

Celery takes 4-5 months to be ready. An acre can yield 9000 kg. of cerely.

## PARSLEY (*Petroselinum crispum*)

### Family : Umbelliferae

Parsley is a native of mediterranean region. It is very popular in the West. Fresh parsley is used in salad. The dry leaves in a powdered form is used to add spicy flavour to the cooked food. Boiled vegetable sprinkled with parsley leaf powder tastes delicious. Parsley contains vitamin C.

For growing parsley 1500 g of seed is required. Seed takes two weeks to germinate. Soil is prepared as for cauliflower. Seedlings are transplanted 20 cm. apart in rows. The distance from row to row should be 45 cm. Seedlings are raised from September to November. The agrotechnique is the same as for celery. The large leaves from the base are picked and consumed.

**Variety:** 'Improved curled'.

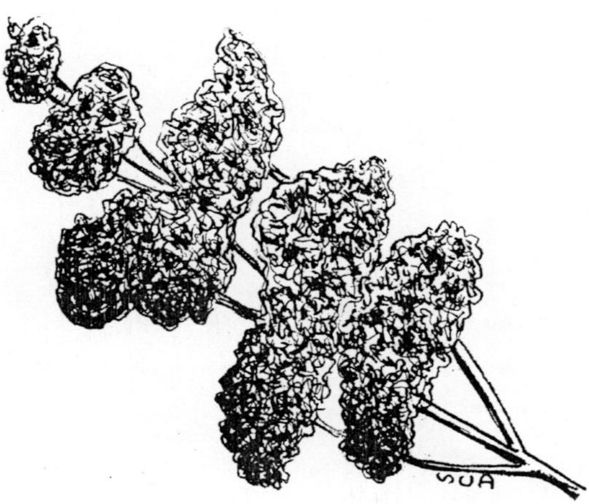

**Fig. 21:** Parsley.

## CRESS (*Lepium sativum*)

### Family : Brassicaceae

**Other names : *Sans.-* Chandrashura; *Hindi-* Halim, *Beng.-* Halim; Aleveri; *Mar.-* Ahliva ; *Guj.-* Asalio, Halim; *Kan.-* Allibija.**

Cress is the native of Iran. It can be grown through all seasons of the year in any soil and climate suitable for agriculture. From July-January cress can be grown in the plains of India successively. It is used as salad and to garnish the dish of food on the table.

Rich and moist soil is suitable for growing cress. The seed requirement for an acre of land is 3 kg. Cress grows first like turnip. Within 3 weeks of sowing leaves are picked for use.

**Varieties:** Common cress can be gown in all seasons. But there is another species (*L. barbarea*) which is known as `Upland Cress'. It is grown only in winter.

## CORIANDER (*Coriandrum sativum*)

### Family : Umbelliferae

**Other names : *Sans.-* Dhanya, Kustumburi; *Hindi-* Dhania; Beng.-Dhane; *Guj.-* Konphir; *Mar.-* Dhanna; *Mal.-* Kothumpalari.**

Coriander leaf is very popular in this country. It is used as salad, for flavouring cooked food and garnishing food dish on the table. The soil preparation is similar to that for radish. Each fruit of coriander which is used as spice has two seeds. So before sowing the fruit should be split to halves and soaked in water for 10-12 hours. On sowing cover the seeds with a thin layer of finely seived friable cow manure. Seed germinates 6-10 days. One month old seedlings are pricked out and put into small bundles for marketing. Then top dressing of urea (10kg) is applied just before irrigation. In the next stage the large leaves are picked to put into bundles.

## MINT (*Mentha arvensis*)

### Family : Labiatae

**Other names: *Bengali, Mar.Guj. and Tel.*- Podina, Pudina, Pudina; Kan.- Chetni maragu.**

The mint is used like coriander. It is a small perennial herb. Mint is easily grown with success. Once planted it supplies the leaves for few years.

The plant is propagated by shoot cuttings or suckers. The cuttings roots within a week. Mint is grown in beds as is done in case of seasonal flowers. A bed of 45 sq.m. (45 cm. x 10 m) is prepared with the following fertilizer mixture.

Humus........................................................ 20 buckets (10 litre cap.)

Hoof and Hornmeal.................................... 5 kg.

Bone meal/Super phosphate....................... 1.5 kg.

Wood ash/muriate of potash ...................... 5 kg.

Plant the rooted cuttings or suckers 30 cm. apart. A monthly dose of 20 g. of urea per sq.m. is applied as top dressing The shoot cuttings of 10 cm. long are put in small bundles for the market. Liquid manure can also be applied with advantage. If it is applied the top dressing of urea should not be used.

# *Perennial Vegetable*

## ASPARAGUS (*Asparagus officinalis*)

**Family : Liliaceae**

Other names : *Hindi and Mar.*- Satavar, Safed-musli; *Guj.*- Ujli-musli; Dholi-musali.

Asparagus is a popular vegetable of the cold countries. It is not grown in the plains. Like common asparagus it has a large bunch of fleshy roots which are perennial. In spring new shoots sprout, which are used as vegetable. Asparagus is a costly vegetable. Once grown the sprouts are harvested for 10-12 years.

Asparagus is propagated by seed. About 200g of seed is required for an acre of land.

The seedlings will grow in the seed bed for a year. In the next spring they are transplanted 45 cm. apart on the ridges. The soil preparation is the same as in the case of onion. The furrow between the ridges are used for irrigation. Top dressing is applied twice at a month's interval in spring and summer. Liquid manure can be used instead. 8-10 quintal sprouts are obtained from an acre of land.

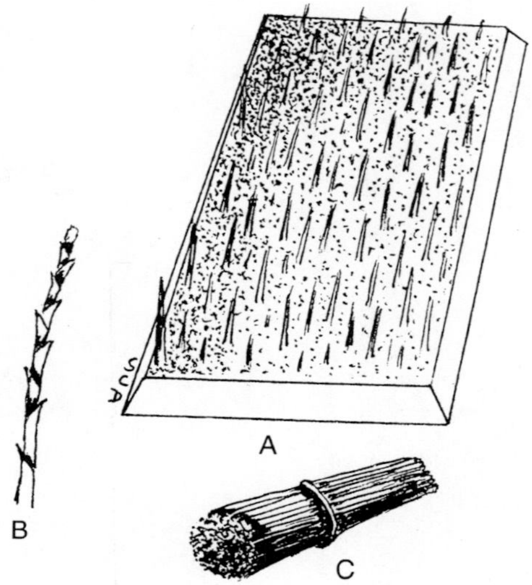


Fig. 22: Asparagus. A. A neat bed, B. A single sprout, C. A bundle of sprout for market.

## GLOBE ARTICHOKE (*Cynara scolymus*)

### Family : Compositae

**Other names:** ***Hindi and Beng.-*** **Hathichak, Hathi choke.**

There is two types of artichoke - one is globe artichoke and the other is Jerusalem artichoke. But they are not related to each other though they belong to the same family (*Compositae*). Because the former is a flower head, whereas the later is a corm-like root which are used as vegetable. So the later has been included in the category of tuberous vegetable.

**Fig. 23:** Globe artichoke

For growing in an acre of land 200g of artichoke seed is required. Seed is sown in the seed bed. Seedlings of 20-25 cm. high are transplanted 20-25 cm. apart in the rows. The distance between the two adjacent rows is 1 m. The flower heads appear at the age of 8-10 months. The flowers in their early stage are used as a fresh or cooked vegetable.

Artichoke is a perennial plant which is also propagated by cuttings or suckers. A crop should last for three years only. Though the plants usually live beyond this period. It needs a very rich soil.

# *Leafy Vegetable*

Leaves and twigs of a good number of species are used as vegetable. They are called `leafy vegetable' or `Pot herb', Every day we should eat some leafy vegetable. It is nutritious, tasty and rich in vitamin and minerals. If taken regularly one can be free from the trouble of constipation. It is grown easily within a very short time. Hence cheap. For any season there are species to suit. Therefore, leafy vegetable is available in all seasons.

## INDIAN SPINACH (*Basella* spp.)

### Family : Basellaceae

**Other names : Hindi, Beng. & Mar-*Poi*; Tel.-*Batsala*; Kan.-*Basale*; Mal.-*Basala*.**

Indian spinach grown in all parts of the country. There are three cultivated types. The most common type being the green basalla with dark green oval leaves, the second type has the leaves and stems of red colour ; the third type has dark green cordate leaves. Amongst the wild types the red variety predominates. In the moist climate of the coastal region of the country basella is found to grow wild. The stems of a wild species are thin and the leaves are small.

The tender shoots, leaves and stems are chopped and cooked as vegetable. The tender shoots, fresh or cooked are rich in vitamins.

Basella grows through all seasons of the year. For the *rabi* crop sow seed in January-February and for the *Kharif* crop it is to be done in April - May. Seed is sown 5 cm. apart on ridges. Its seedlings like those of radish should be thinned out successively. The tender plants have good demand in the market.

The stems are thick but week which grow trailing on the ground. In kitchen gardens the vines are given support of a inclined pergola. That stands at an angle of 30° to the ground. The lower and end of the pergola should touch the ground near the base of the plants grown in rows. In the places of heavier rainfall the support should be provided for the stems of the *Kharif* crop.

Though the crop is seasonal even one-year old thick stems remain green. Hence edible. So the vines are cut into pieces of 45 cm. long and put into bundles for the market.

The plants of the *Kharif* put forth bud-shaped bloosoms of green, white and pink colours which are also used as vegetable. The blossoms come up on the eve of winter, in that stage the plant itself becomes sour in taste. Hence not edible.

The cultural process is very simple. The plant need more nitrogen and irrigation. In the shortage of nitrogen the quality of the vegetable deteriorates.

## SPINACH (*Spinacia oleracea*)

### Family : Chinopodiacea

**Other names : Hindi-*Isfanaj, Palak*; Bengali-*Palang*; Mar. & Guj.-*Palak*, Tel.-*Dumpabachhali*.**

Spinach is also known as `Beet leaf'. It is very popular in the eastern region of the country, especially in West Bengal and also in Bangla Desh. It is however, not liked by the people of the southern states. Spinach can be grown in any type of soil having sufficient fertility and proper drainage system. But sandy loam is preferred most. It grows well in a $p^H$ 6.5-7.5. In the plains it is grown from October to February. In the mild climate it can be grown throughout the year. The crop is frost-tolerant and also tolerates warm weather.

Normally seeds are sown by broadcasting at the rate of 10 kg/acre.

The sowing of pre-soaked seeds is in practice. For this, soak the seeds in water for a week or so before sowing. Seed germinates in a week.

## AMARANTHUS (*Amranthus blitum* Var. *oleracea*)

### Family : Amarantaceae

**Other names : *Sans.-* Marisha; *Hindi-* Chaulai; Marsa; *Beng.*-Marish, Sadanotye; *Mar.-* Bhaji; Guj.-Dambho; *Tel.-* Totakura; *Tam.-* Tandukirai.**

Small plants with stems and leaves are used as leafy vegetable. When they grow tall the stems are cooked and consumed like drumsticks. Stems contain enough carbohydrates and minerals. The vegetable as pot herb is rich in vitamin and minerals.

The species has many varieties. All of them are grown in the plains throughout the year, i.e. either as a *rabi* or *kharif* crop. It can stand the mild winter, extreme heat and heavy rains of the plains. Therefore seed can be sown any time of the year. Seed is sown in long beds of short width of 60cm. In the early stage the seedlings are pricked out and put into bundles for the market.

For growing stem vegetable the seedlings are transplanted 20 cm. apart in rows on the ridges especially for the *kharif* crop. The distance from row to row should be 45 cm. Start the process of thinning out when the plants grow to a height of 45 cm. As the plants grow larger more space for spreading is required. The large plants with large and thick branches weighing about 2-3 kg each are in a great demand in the market.

Six weeks after transplanting top-dressing of urea (15 kg/acre) should be applied. In the basal dressing the amount of potash and phosphate should be more than usual.

## FENUGREEK (*Trigonella foenum-graecum*)

### Family : Leguminosae

**Other names : Hindi-*Methi, Muthi*; Beng.-*Methi, Methi Shak*; Guj.-*Methi, Methini*; Mal.-*Uluva*.**

The leaves and twigs are used as a pot herb and seed is a scented spice. It is a vegetable of cold weather. Because it is frost tolerant. Fenngreek is a highly nutritious vegetable.

Sow seed in the seed bed as in the case of amaranthus. The seedlings of 10-15 cm. high is pricked out and put in the bundles for the market. The deficiency of nitrogen will deteriorate the quality of the vegetable.

## PIRING (*Trigonella corniculata*)

### Family : Leguminosae

**Other names : Hindi-*Kesuri methi*; Beng.-*Piring*; Rajasthan-*Chirawa*; Assam-*Piring* sak.**

The plant resembles methi, but does not grow erect. The taste is bitter. Still it is used as a pot herb.

## LEAFY ONION (*Allium fisturosum*)

### Family : Liliaceae

**Other names : *Eng.- Ceboule, Welsh onion; Beng.- Pat pyanj, Pyanj shak.***

The plant resembling onion does not form bulb and grow in a compact clump. The leaf cuttings are used as a vegetable. It is very soft and tasty. The besal part of the plant that grows just above the fibrous roots is also used. The taste of the vegetable is like that of onion. The blanched basal part also used as salad. Raising seedlings, transplanting and after-care are the same as for onion (see Bulb vegetable).

## WATER SPINACH (*Convolvulus reptans*, syn.-*Ipomoea replans*)

### Family : Convolvulaceae

**Other names: *Eng.- Swamp cabbage, Water spinach; Hindi- Sarnali, Ganthian; Beng.- Kalmisag; Mar.- Nadishaka, Guj.- Nalanibhaji; Tel.- Tutikura, Tam.- Vellaikeerai.***

An aquatic herb. Long vine-like stems float on water. Internodes are hollow, like a tube that contains air and help float on water. The tender twigs are used as vegetable which is very delicious and nutritious. It is a popular vegetable of the region where ponds and marshes are abundant. *Kalmisag* is a summer vegetable. It is available from March to September in West Bengal. The climate of the southern states is ideal for its growth.

Previously the supply was from the natural vegetation. Due to its popularity, the demand has increased immensely. So it is cultivated in the field as well in the kitchen garden. Seed is now available in the market. The beds of few contimetre deep from the ground level should be prepared using a basal dressing of humus 50 kg. per 10 sq.m. together with 1 kg. of super phosphate and 600g of muriate of potash. Cutting should be started when the shoots grow to a length of 30cm. The successive cuttings become ready at an interval of 2 weeks. After each cutting top dressing of 1 kg. of urea per 100 sq. m should be applied. Due to the shortage of nitrogen the quality of the vegetable will deteriorate. If seeds are not available the shoot cuttings collected from the marsh or market can be planted directly in the field. The seeds are sown or cuttings are planted in February-March.

## CURRYLEAF (*Murraya koenigli*)

### Family: Rutaceae

**Other names: *Sans.-* Surabhininiba; *Hindi-* Kurry patta, Mitha neem; *Beng.-* Barsanga; *Tel-* Karepaku; *Tam.-* Karivempu; *Guj.-* Goranimb; *Oriya-* Barsan.**

A large shrub or small is tree cultivated in Tamil Nadu, Maharestra and North India. Leaves are used for flavouring curries as well as making *pokorda*.

The plant is also popular as an ornamental. In the most part of the country it is found in the kitchen garden. It is easily grown from seeds or cuttings.

# *Kitchen Gardening*

The part of the home garden used to grow vegetables is called `Kitchen garden'. Generally the frontyard is utilized for flowers or other ornamentals, and the backyard is allocated for fruits and vegetables. Obviously the housewives are very keen in growing vegetable for the kitchen. It is perhaps for having fresh vegetable at their command. Secondly they have not to depend entirely on the market that cannot always supply you fresh vegetable. Fresh and crisp vegetable are more nutritious than the state and desiccated ones.

Kitchen gardening is not motivated with a view to saving money rather than finding a scope for pre-occupation in the pursuit of growing nutritious food through the joy of creation. Secondly in summer the supply is lean in the market just contrary to winter. Then one has to depend more on one's kitchen garden.

The *rabi* and pre-*kharif* crops demand more water for irrigation. For this period if water is wanting the selection of the species and the varieties should be such as to managing them with less water. Not only that the quantity of the crop must be reduced. Clay soil demands less irrigation, because its water retentivity is high. The main characteristic of kitchen gardening is to provide many species rather than a few in quantities. The emphasis should be laid in maintaining a balanced ratio among the subjects.

A kitchen garden can be raised in ground or pot. Due to the obvious reasons the pot culture has its limitations. But those who cannot but resort to roof top gardening have to grow vegetable in pots.

## GROUND CULTURE

If the ground space is sufficient some fruit vegetables like drumstick (moringa), vegetable banana, papaya etc. can be accomodated. Pumpkin, bottle gourd, flat beans also need a large space for the spreading vines. On the other hand brinjal, chilli, tomato, cabbage, cauliflower, radish, carrot, elephant foot etc. can be grown in a small space. Vegetable cannot be grown in a shady place. Therefore the trees with spreading head should not stand on the eastern and southern side of the garden. But if they stand on the northern and western sides the shade cast by them in the afternoon do not cause any harm. Because the sunshine from morning to afternoon (upto 3 p.m.) is considered sufficient for growing vegetable. But their roots likely to encroach the site for your vegetable. If so happens make a ditch of 45 cm. deep along the border of the site demarcated for your vegetable so that root running horizentally cannot cross the ditch.

For the shady corner of the garden some species of vegetable can be tried. They are pumpkin, bitter gourd, chilli etc. Bitter gourd can be trained to the grill of back verandah. The vines of the cucurbits grown in the shade can be trained to the area having enough sunlight.

## ROOF-TOP GARDEN

Due to the want of space for gardening vegetable can be grown as pot plants. The verandah, roof top or front terrace can be used for placing the pots. The halves of an iron drum, packing crates (wooden) with open top wooden rats etc. can be used as containers. In the urban areas ground space for vegetables are scarce. Still it cannot dampen the enthusiasm. For the urban people the provision is also there in the flower shows to compete the exhibits of pot vegetables. For vegetable the large flower pots are used. The rings for burnt clay which are meant for lining wells or soak pits can be conveniently used for terrace gardening with vegetables. On crocking the drain hole at the bottom of the flowerpots should be filled with potting compost. An empty space of 2-3 cm deep should be there at the top to hold water of watering. Then seeds are sown or seedlings are planted as usual.

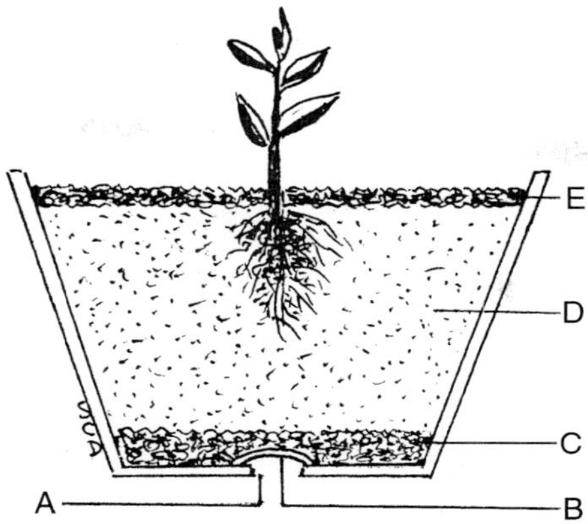


**Fig. 24:** A seedling in a pot. A. Drain hole, B. Crock, C. A layer of grit and sand, D. Compost, E. Mulch.

## POTTING COMPOST

1. Loam ........................................ 10 buckets (10 litre cap.)
   Cow manure/compost ........................ 3 buckets
   Urea ........................................ 200 g.
   Super phosphate ............................ 250 g.
   Muriate of potash .......................... 200 g.
   Magnesium sulphate ......................... 20 g.

2. Humus ....................................... 4 buckets
   Urea ........................................ 150g
   Super phosphate ............................ 200g
   Muriate of potash .......................... 175 g
   Magnesium sulphate ......................... 20 g.

3. Heavy soil (Clay) .......................... 10 buckets
   Humus ....................................... 4 buckets
   Hoof and hornmeal .......................... 1 kg.

Super phosphate ........................................ 200g.
Muriate of potash ...................................... 150g.
Magnesium sulphate .................................. 20 g.
Chalk dust ................................................. 50 g.

4. Loam ........................................................ 10 buckets
Humus ....................................................... 3 buckets
Suphala 15:15:15 ....................................... 400g

5. Loam ........................................................ 10 buckets
Humus ....................................................... 3 buckets
DAP (Di-ammonium Phosphate) ............. 300g
Muriate of Potash ...................................... 150 g.

6. Loam ........................................................ 10 Buckets
Humus ....................................................... 3 buckets
Iffco 10:26:26 ............................................ 300g.

7. Humus ...................................................... 10 buckets
Gromor 28:28:0 ......................................... 3 buckets
Muriate of potash ...................................... 200 g.

8. Loam ........................................................ 10 buckets
Humus ....................................................... 3 buckets
Sterameal/Rallimeal .................................. 300g.

9. Loam ........................................................ 10 buckets
Humus ....................................................... 3 buckets
Oilcake (*Neem*/mustard/ground nut) ......... 300 g
Urea ......................................................... 50 g
Super phosphate ........................................ 250g.
Muriate of potash ...................................... 100g.

10. Loam ........................................................ 10 buckets
Humus........................................................ 3 buckets
Oilcake (*Neem*).......................................... 350 g.
Urea .......................................................... 50g.
Super phosphate ....................................... 250 g
Muriate of potash ..................................... 100g.

11. Loam ........................................................ 10 buckets
Humus........................................................ 3 buckets
Floramix...................................................... 200 g.

Any of the above mixture can be used as potting compost for pot vegetables. The mixture no 9 and 10 contain oil cake which must be decomposed before use. Mix first three ingredients and keep it in a moist condition in a heap for three weeks. Then mix the other ingredients and use as potting compost.

When the deficiency symptoms will be shown the food supplements in the form of top dressing or liquid manure should be applied.

For the large plants of cucurbits, e.g. pumpkin, ash gourd, bottle gourd etc. comparatively big pots are required. The container containing 75-100L of soil should be used.

For the *rabi* or pre-*kharif* crops waterinbg is required daily. On the contrary the *kharif* crop is rain-fed. If there is no rain for a few consecutive days no watering is required usually, because the humid air helps maintain the moisture level of the soil for days together. Other operations are the same as for the ground plants.

The soil of the pot should be changed every year. If it is not possible sterilize the soil with the use of formalin. It is available in the market with the strength of 40%.

To treat the soil prepare a solution of formalin. Add 40 ml of the chemical to a litre of water. Drench the soil with the solution. Keep it in a heap which should be covered with a sheet of polythene. After 48 hours remove the cover The soil can be used when the formalin gas will escape completely from the treated soil.

# *Pest and Disease Control*

## PESTS

To check the insect attack the effective remedy is found in the application of insecticides. As the vegetable is consumed the insecticide harmful to human life should not be used especially when the vegetable (leaves, shoots or fruits) are picked. One month before picking the strong chemical insecticide can be used. Therefore in the early stage vegetable plants can be protected by applying insecticides.

The large insects which can be picked by hand should be destroyed by hand picking. There are certain insecticides which are not harmful to man can be used safely as required. The process of preparation of those insecticides are appended in the last. The chemical ingredients of fungicides are less harmful to man and animal. The active principles of the insecticides can be removed by simply washing the vegetable. the sulfur or lime based fungicides, e.g. wettable sulfur. Lime sulfur, Bordeaux mixture, Burgandy mixture, sulfur dust etc. are not harmful. They can be removed by washing.

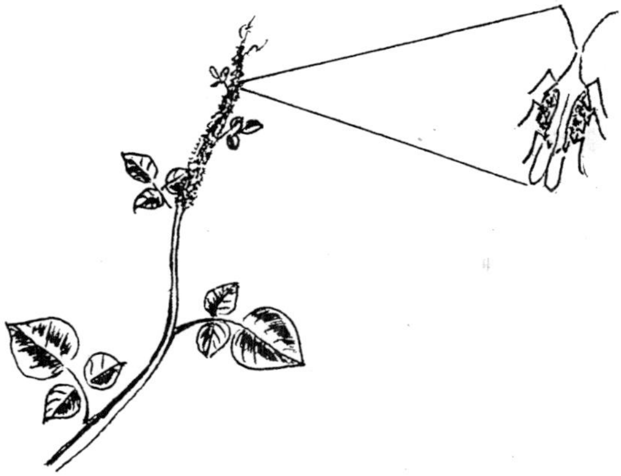

Fig. 25: The shoot of bean infested with Aphid. One of them is magnified.

## Fruit Borer

The larvae bore into the fruits of Okra, tomato etc. Collect and destroy the damaged fruits. Spray *neem* emulsion.

*Chemical control* - Metacid 50 (2 ml/L) or Endosel (2ml/L) Spray.

## Shoot and Fruit Borer

It is a serious trouble found in growing brinjal. The small caterpillars bore into the twigs and fruits. Remove the affected parts of the plant and destroy by burning.

*Chemical control* - Spraying of Endosel (2ml/L) at an interval of 12-15 days. The granular systemic insecticides like Furadam-3G, Thimet -10G (Phorate 10G) etc. can be applied (2g/Sq m.) in the soil. The roots will absorb the chemical to protect them from inside. Their use is recommended in the pre-fruiting stage.

## Thrips

The minute insects suck the sap from leaves which curl and dry at tips. This trouble is common in chillis.

*Chemical contro -* Spraying of tobacco-leaf emulsion (See Appendix) or Nicotine sulphate (1.5ml/L) or Malathion (2m/L) or sevin (500g/acre) or Rogor (2m/L).

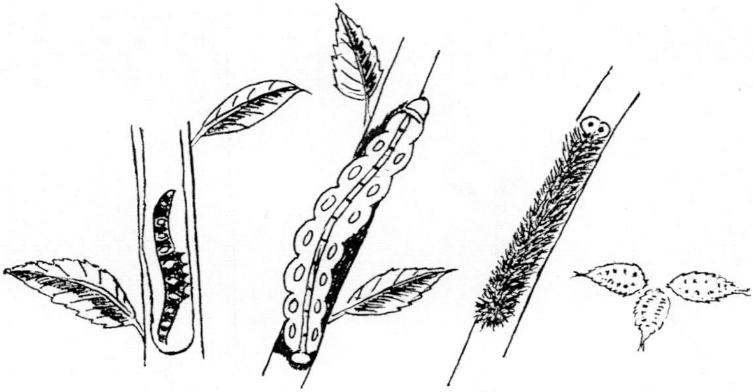

A B C D

**Fig. 26:** Pests. A. Stem borer, B. Caterpillar, C. Hairy caterpiller, D. Mealy bugs.

## Aphids

Black or brown small winged insects come in thousands and suck the sap of the growing tips and soft foliage of radish, beans, cowpeas etc. Spraying of tobacco-leaf emulsion controls the insect (See Appendix).

*Chemical Control-* Malathion (2 ml/L spray.)

## Jassids

They suck the sap from the lower surface of the leaves and inject some toxic substance resulting in curling of leaves upwards and the plant growth is stunted.

*Chemical control -* Monocil (2ml/L) spray, or Endosel (2ml/L) spray.

## Mites

The minute insects remain in the lower surface of the leaves and suck their sap resulting in the pale-yellow appearance.

*Chemical control* - Dusting the plants with flour of Sulfur (25g/10 sq.m.) or spraying cold water on the lower surface of the leaves.

## Potato Tuber Moth

Brownish grey insects with minute dark markings in the forewings. The larvae of the insect damage the tubers. It is a major pest of potato in storage.

To prevent the trouble use healthy tubers as seed. Secondly earthing should be thick to cover the growing tubers. If they are exposed or peep through the soil the moth will lay eggs on them. The chemical control is not advised as it poisons the vegetable.

## Leaf Eating Caterpillars

They feed voraciously on leaves. Collecting and destroying the egg messes and hand picking of the large individuals are an effective control.

*Chemical control* : Metacid-50 (2ml/L) or Malathion (2ml/L) or Monocil (2ml/L) spray.

## Mealy Bugs

A soft bodied insect covered with a white or brown powder - like substance suck the sap from the tender parts of the plant. They secret a honey-like substance from their body which attracts the ants. The adults hardly move. Infestation spreads mainly by ants.

Collect the egg-masses deposited on the leaves and destroy. The adults should be removed by hand-picking.

*Chemical control*-Malathion (2ml/L) or Metasystocks (1m/L) spray.

## Red Pumpkin Beetles

They cause a serious damage to cucurbits especially at the young stage. Small flying insects of orange colour perch on the leaves in bright sunshine and feed on the leaves. Spraying of *Neem* emulsion can repulse the insects. The leaf extract of *Ashshoura* (*Glycosmis pentaphylla*) if sprayed with water (30ml./L) can check the attack effectively.

*Chemical control* - Malathion (2ml/L) spray.

### Nematodes

Root-knot nematodes and reniform nematodes are found to effect papaya. The effected plants becomes stunted in growth, the leaves show yellowish colour.

*Control* - Furadan 3G (2g/sq m) , soil application.

### Banana Stem Borer

This insect cause much damage to banana plants. The grubs bore into the stem. The leaves become yellow and consequently the plant dies.

*Control* - Placing of celphos tablets (3 for each plant) inside the stem and plastering the slit with mud.

### Fig Stem Borer

The grubs bore into the stems and cause damage therein.

*Control* - Put few drops of kerosene oil in the hole and plug the hole with cotton soaked in kerosene.

### Hairy Caterpillars

They are common in drumstick plants in autumn to early winter. The insects feed on the foliage at night. In the morning they are found congregated on the lower part of the stem. Control - Malathion (2ml/L) spray.

### Cabbage Caterpillars

The white butterfly lays egg on the cabbage. They hatch into caterpillars that bore into cabbage head and cause damage by feeding on foliage. *Control* - Dust 4% sevin on the plants.

### Garden Centipedes

The insects feed on the underground bulbs and tubers. The perennial root vegetables like asparagus is damaged by centipedes. They are very fond of fasciculated and fleshy roots of the plant.

*Control* - Dust sevin near the plants and kill the insects.

### White Grubs

The adult grubs lay eggs in the soil. Their presence in light soil is common.

*Control* - Soil application of Thimet 10G or Phorate 10G (100G/100sq.m) before planting.

## Termites

They are attracted by the organic substances of the soil. Termites destroy soil humus and then roots and stems of the plants.

*Control* - Soil dressing with B.H.C., Aldrin or D.D.T. - The liquid chemicals like Darsban or Pyriban can be used against termites.

## Mole Crickets (Gryllotalp vulgaris)

They cause harm to seeds and seedlings. They are attracted by organic matters of the soil. They make burrows as they pass just below the soil surface.

*Control* - As recommended against termites.

## Earthworms

They cause harm to many *kharif* crops. The earthworm multiplies in soil with plenty of humus. The young individuals feed on the growing roots and the injury caused thereby is susceptible to the disease infection.

*Control* - As recommended against termites.

The application of *Mahua* oilcake in the diluted form can destroy earthworms. The solution of permanganate of potash can be applied to kill earthworms. The granular insecticides like Furadan, Phorate etc. are very poisonous to earthworms. It is obvious that the application of *Mahua* oil cake or permanganate of potash is safe for vegetable.

# DISEASES

## Damping Off

Soil-borne fungi attack the seedlings at the collar region in the seed bed or seed pan. The congested seedlings are very susceptible to this disease. The affected seedlings collapsed. *Control* - Treating the seed with Ceresan (2g/kg) before sowing. Drenching soil with the suspension of Captan or Brassical (2g/L).

### Blight

A soil borne disease. Leaves and Stems are destroyed by the fungous attack. The dark, water soaked spots on the stems and fungus spores on the underside of the leaves are the symptoms. The disease spreads in a cloudy weather. It may be a menace to potato field.

*Control* - Weekly spraying of Dithane M-45 (2.5g/L). Treating the seed potato with fungicides.

### Fruit Rot

The tender fruits of tomato or cucurbits rot when infected by the disease. First black or brown spots appear on the immature fruits.

*Control* - Treating seed with Thiram or Captan (2.5g/kg of seed) and spraying plants with Difolatan (3g/L).

### Fusarium Wilt

A seed-borne disease. First the lower leaves wilt and eventually the plants. It is very common in tomato.

*Control* - Using seed of resistant varieties. Treating seed with Agrosan GN or Thiram (2.5g/kg of seed) and spraying plants with Dithane (M-45 (2.5g/l) at weekly intervals.

### Bacterial Wilt

The infected plants become stunted and then wilt. It is a seed-borne disease. Collect and destroy the plants.

*Control* - Using healthy seed and seedlings. Treating seed with hot water at 50°C for 25 minutes before sowing.

### Powdery Mildew

White powdery growth on the leaves. The infected leaves rot.

*Control* - Spraying of sulfur - based fungicides like lime-sulphur, Wettable sulfur, Sulfex, Sulphatox etc.

### Anthracnose

Circular spots develop on fruits or stems. The affected branch dries and fruits drop. It is common in chillies.

*Control* - Spraying of Dithane-M (45 (2g/L), Blue copper (3g/L) and Difoltan (2g/L) alternately at a week interval.

## Black Rot

It is a disease of sweet potato. Both vines and tubers are affected. Vines wilt and black spot appear on tubers.

*Control* - Selecting healthy tubers and vines for planting. Treating the vines with Aretan or Agallol before planting.

## Black Spot

The infected leaves show brown or black spots. They expand and the leaves rot.

*Control* - Spraying of Dithane-M 45 (2g/L) twice or thrice at the interval of 10-15 days.

## Rust

Small white slightly raised spots are found on the lower surface of the leaves. These turn dark brown to black.

*Control* - Just like that of Powdery mildew.

## Downy Mildew

The affected part looks like wet cotton and slimy. The affected parts rot immediately.

*Cotrol* - Spraying of Dithane - M 45 (2g/L).

# VIRAL DISEASES

The plant affected with vires are practically damaged and there is no cure. The disease is spread by insects especially the tiny flies. If flies are destroyed by spraying insecticides the virus cannot spread rapidly. Secondly the virus infected plants must not be used as planting materials. If these precautions are adopted the spread of vires can be checked effectively.

### Mosaic Virus

The common symptoms of attack are mottling, chlorosis (yellowing), Vein-banding and blistering of the leaf surfaces. Very common in papaya, cucurbits and okra.

*Control* - Destroying the affected parts/plants. Spraying of insecticides like Thiodan (1g/L) or Metasystox (1g/L) to destroy the flies.

### Leaf curl

The leaves are thickened and curl inwards resulting in the stunted growth. It occurs commonly in Papaya. *Control*- Same as mosaic virus.

### Bunchy Top

The leaves become short and leaf blade narrow. All leaves appear in a bunch. The growth becomes stunted. *Control*- Same as mosaic virus.

## SEED DRESSING WITH FUNGICIDES

Seed is treated with fungicides to remove seed-borne diseases. The small quantity seed is treated in a plastic jar conveniently. For the large quantities the seed dresser is used. For dressing purpose various chemicals are available in the markets.

- **Agrosan G.N.:** It is a mercury-based fungicide which is used extensively for treating seed. Only 3g of the chemical is needed to treat one kg of seed. The seeds thus treated should not be consumed. While using cover the nose and mouth with a piece of cloth.
- **Formaldehyde:** It is very effective to remove scab and smut diseases of potato. Mix 550 ml. of formaldehyde (40%) with 250 L of water. Spray the solution on the seed potato. Cover the treated seed with a sheet of polythene for 4-5 hours.
- **Dithane M-45:** Soak the seed or seedlings in a suspension of 2.5g of Dithane with one litre of water for 20-30 minutes. When the liquid will dries up sow the seed or transplant the seedlings.
- **Agallol 6:** It prevents the blight, scab and Fusorium wilt of potato. Potato seed, whole or divided, is treated with the solution (1.5 g/L) for 3-5 minutes.

- **Bavistin:** To prevent many seed-borne fungous diseases seed is treated with the solution of this systemic fungicide (1g/L) for 3-4 minutes.
- **Agrimycin:** To prevent bacterial diseases like wilting, foot rotting etc. treat the potato seed by dipping in a solution (1.5 ml/L) for few minutes. Plantomycin can also be used instead.
- **Hot Water:** It can prevent the black spot of cole crops. Soak the seed in a hot water of 50°C for 10 minutes. It can kill the germ lying under the skin of the seed.

## TOXICITY OF PESTICIDES IN VEGETABLES

The pests destroy the crop which causes the loss to the farmers and the shortage of food to the nation. So it becomes imperative to use pesticides to kill or ward off the pests. But their toxicity may linger to reach our stomach. Therefore one must have the understanding as to the toxicity of pesticides applied. This toxicity is far -reaching. For example, green fodder is protected from the pest by applying poisonous insecticides. But the toxicity of some pesticides is so long lasting that the active principle of the poison has been traced in the milk of the cow. The consumers of such milk will surely be affected by the poison. The same thing is likely to happen in case of vegetable. The following precautions have to be taken against the danger.

The chemical should be measured correctly with the help of a measure glass.

For the understanding of all a board mentioning the use of pesticide must be put in the field so that owner of the cattle and goats prevent their animals from browsing and the pilferers can restrain themselves from pouching the poisonous vegetables.

Generally, long before reaching the picking condition the strong insecticides are used. It must be stopped at least a week before the picking starts.

Mild insecticides or fungicides are not so harmful and for this reason the aforesaid restrictions are not usually imposed. In the Appendix the preparation of some mild insecticide and safe fungicides have been given.

# Appendix: A

## THE ROLE OF VEGETABLE AND OTHER FOODS IN PREVENTING DISEASES

In the nutritional research it has been found that some food can prevent or cure certain deadly diseases. There are such foods that can cure even certain heart troubles. The experiments have proved that certain foods can prevent even the deadly disease like cancer.

Food not only satisfy our hunger it also causes the all-round development of our body and mind, and prevent or cure ailments which are not caused by infection. Fish is more nutritious than meat. Similarly brown eggs have more food valve than the white ones. But vegetable is considered best.

The modern research has proved that 40g. of oat-bran (*Isabgul*) if taken daily 20% of lipoprotein cholesterol of low density will be reduced. This type of cholesterol chokes the passage through the arteries thus causing the heart trouble. Oat bran gradually removes the harmful low density lipoprotein (LDL) cholesterol and increases the high density lipoprotein cholesterol which is helpful to the normal functioning of the blood circulation. Besides gram, lentil (*mung*) and red cow pea (Kidney bean or *Rajmah*) if taken regularly cholesterol trouble of the blood can be removed. Other foods which are equally useful in this respect are apple, barley (grain), carrot, brinjal, skimmed milk and the beverage prepared from fatless curd (*Ghole*). For example, if 2-3 apples are eaten daily 10 per cent of harmful cholesterol is checked.

One should not depend entirely on meat protein. Fifty per cent of the total protein requirement of the body should be met by the protein from the vegetable sources, i.e. mainly from pulses. The protein from soyabean helps reduce the harmful cholesterol of the blood. The half of an onion, if taken daily, increases the high density cholesterol which is useful to the normal blood circulation. The persons having the cholesterol trouble should never take crustacean food like crab, snail and prawn. Because these help increase the low density lipoprotein cholesterol.

In 1981 Richard poll and Richard Petro told that the death by cancer in America has been reduced to 60 per cent by changing diets. They are hopeful that the future research will find out the efficacy of certain food to prevent the cancer of stomach, gall bludder, ovary, breast and pancreas. The role of fibre portion of vegetables, fruits, and cereals are not digested. It is considered roughage portion of the food. Fat or fat-rich food is very tasty that is why one is tempted to have such food. But one should refrain from eating much fat especially that obtained from the animal sources.

It has been found that those who eat more vegetable are almost free from the cancer of chest, colon and prostate. Vegetable-rich food makes the bones hard. Radish, cabbage, cauliflower kholkhol and carrot are anti carcinogenic. In other words they contain some chemical substances known as Indole that becomes active on protein cells to cause cancer the anticarcinogenic substances reduce its toxicity. These vegetables have another property that prevents cancer by bringing about some changes in cytochrome P-450 a colouring matter of blood. The U.S. National Research Council recommends that the daily dietary must include cabbage, cauliflower, brussel sprout, knol-khol, turnip, radis, mustard leaf, rape leaf etc. etc. The N.R.C. has found out that the food rich in carotinoids reduces the possibilities of cancer. Carotinoids together with vitamin A have a great role in preventing cancer and these are available in fruits and vegetables of deep yellow colour (Plum, carrot etc.) and deep green leafy vegetables (*Palak*, *poi* etc.). Milk, liver and yolk are rich in vitamin A. Two Japanese scientists have discovered that the white portion of an egg contains lumiclavin and lumicrome that prevent cancer effectively.

In the old age electron-free atoms (free radicals) develop in human bodies, which is prevented by vitamin C and E. These vitamins are available in oils obtained from soyabean, safflower, cotton seed and in hydrogenated oil, peanut, pod vegetable, breast milk and green leafy vegetables. Citrus fruits contain 27%, potato and sweet potato 14% and green and yellow vegetables 11% of vitamin C.

Due to smoking electron-free atoms develop in the body and carotinoids can save the smoker from this danger. If any atom is oxidised its electron becomes free. The oxidising agents and the electron-free atoms are encircled and guarded by carotinoids thus preventing them from causing any harmful change in the body. The want of selenium in our food may cause cancer. We get selenium from meat, sea food and cereals.

The scientists have identified some foods, the intake of which in a large amount causes cancer. Those are salt-rich pickle, smoked food, fat-rich food etc. Fat-rich milk, red meat, butter, icecream if consumed in large quantities enhance the possibilities of cancer in chest and colon. One should be careful that one should not obtain more than 30 per cent of calories from fat. Addiction to wine may cause cancer of mouth and small intestine. Alcohol-addicted person should not smoke. Moulded food (fungus infected) should not be taken. Because mould develop a toxic substance known as alflatoxin that may be the cause of cancer in stomach, liver and kidney. For this reason stale loaf and peas with fungus growth are harmful.

To cure tuberculosis the physicians administer food rich in vitamin C. that will increase vitamin C in the blood. The more vitamin C will increase in the blood the more rapidly the disease (tuberculosis) will be cured. In this respect the food rich in vitamin C is equally important like medicine. Orange and aonla contain vitamin C in a large amount. The juice of aonla contains vitamin C twenty times more than that of orange. The pickle of aonla or dry preserve of the fruit if kept more than a year its vitamin content decreases considerably. In 1989 America imported the huge quantity of aonla. To cure diabetis food with plenty of fibre is very useful. One should however, clearly know what is fibre. What we get in a large amount from one's food are carbohydrates. These carbohydrates are divided into starch and sugar. They are completely digested in our stomach. Besides there is another type of suff which is not digested. The juice of orange or carrot is very nutritious. But the nutritive substance remains in the fibre. When juice is extracted from orange the fibre is separated. On the contrary when carrot is eaten both fibre and its juice is taken. Flour and fine rice have very little fibre whereas whole wheat (*atta*) has plenty of fibre. While making flour the wheat bran is separated. But it remains in *atta*. Hence fibrous. Fibre adds to the quantitative value of a food. Fibreless food is digested early but it helps little to move bowels.

Therefore fibre is good for health. Two British scientists named J.Tomlin and L.W. Reed made an experiment to determine the utility of fibre in our food. They mixed artificial fibre (pulverized plastic) with the food having no fibre. The result was the same as a fibrous food in the human bodies. The bacteria in the stomach break the fibre into the minute pieces that increase the volume of stool. Besides fibre absorbs the acid secreted from the gall bladder and other harmful minerals and chemical substances developed in the body. When bacteria break the fibre by fermention a kind of fatty acid is developed that check the formation of harmful cholesterol in blood. Two British physicians (D.P. Barkit and T.L. Clid) explained in 1973 that the people of a developing country like Africa are almost free from the heart disease as their food contains plenty of fibre. The people of the underdeveloped areas of Asia and Africa get more than 20 per cent of fibre through their food. Barkit and Clid further added that the people of Europe and America take food containing very less fibre and this is the reason why the heart attacks so common in these continents. In pregnancy or in old age if once the heart is attacked the remedy lies in the use of more fibre-rich food. To prevent the cancer of colon the role of fibre is doubtless. Some salts are secreted from the gall bladder which suffer a change due to the bacterial activity in the colon forming a chemical substance known as `Carcinogen'. It is the carcinogen that causes cancer in the body. The scientist K.W. Heaton says that 25-50 percent if gall stone patients of the western countries happen to be due to the less intake of fibrous food. Those Americans who suffer from the coronary trouble happen to be not accomstomed with food having fibre. For the sake of experiment some Africans were fed with the American diets. In course of time they became fatty and fell victim to the coronary disease.

The role of fibre in food essential for maintaining a good health has been proved beyond doubt. Now questions arise how much fibre our food should contain and in what type of food that quantity of fibre is easily available.

The main principle of preventing diseases by the use of fibre being to remove the constipation. One should be habituated with that type of food which help move the bowel regularly. For this reason the dietary must include whole wheat (*atta*) and coarse rice instead of flour and fine rice. Wheat bran and oat bran contain more fibre than any other food stuff. It is better if you can take 2 teaspoonfuls of wheat bran daily. From 4 pieces of bread of whole wheat you can obtain 30 grams of fibre whereas 4 cups of coarse rice (not boiled) contain four grams of fibre. In the dietary you should increase carbohydrates and reduce fat especially of the animal source. Those who are not accustomed to fibre-rich food they should not increase the intake of fibre suddenly. Because this may create the digestive problem.

# Appendix B

## SOME PREPARATIONS

### Bordeaux Mixture

It is the first fungicide developed long ago and was used in the grape fields. But till today it proves to be useful.

Copper sulphate (Blue Vitriol).................... 100g.
Quick lime (CaO) ....................................... 100g.
Water........................................................... 10 L

Take 5 litres of water in a plastic bucket and dissolve copper sulphate in it. In an another bucket take 5 litres of water and soak the lime to form calcium hydroxide (slaked like). Mix the contents of the buckets together and stir for few minutes. Dip a shaving blade into the liquid. It gets rusty if the concentration of copper sulphate is more. To correct it add a little lime. Bordeaux mixture is a very cheap and effective contact fungicide. But it is not so popular for the reasons that it cannot be preserved for the next use. Secondly it leaves a stain on the leaves which cannot be removed easily.

### Lime-Sulphur

It is a very good contact fungicide. After pruning a spraying with lime-sulphur is very effective against the dormant fungus spores. To ward off the attack of mildews and spider mites lime-sulphur is highly recommended.

Sulfur (*Gandhak*) dust ................................ 100 g
Quick lime (CaO) ...................................... 100 g
Water ......................................................... 7.5 L

Take two litres of water in a wooden vat and soak the lime in it. When the temperature will rise to a great extent add sulfur dust to the liquid and stir until the temperature comes down. Then add the rest of water and strain the liquid through a nylon mosquito netting. When cooled spray the liquid and do not preserve it for the next use.

## Nicotine Sulphate

It is very effective against aphids and the like.

Nicotine sulphate (40%) ........................... 25 g
Quick lime (CaO) ..................................... 400 g.

Soak the lime in a pot with its lid. Add nicotine sulphate to it and put the lid. Move the pot gently to mix the ingredients thoroughly.

OR

This mixture is a good substitute of nicotine sulphate.

Dry tobacco leaf......................................... 50 g.
Water ......................................................... 1 L
Washing soap.............................................. 25 g.

Get a decoction by boiling tobacco leaf for an hour. then add soap and stir the liquid until it dissolves. When cooled add 3-4 litres of water and spray on plants.

## Neem Oil Emulsion

*Neem* Oil ..................................................... 40 ml.
Washing soap.............................................. 5 g.
Hot Water.................................................. 6 L

Get the soap dissolved in hot water and then add *neem* oil to it. Stir the mixture for half an hour. The emulsion may be sprayed to prevent common pests.

## Sulfur Dust

As a laboratory chemical pure elemental sulfur (*Gandhak*) in a finely dust form is available in the chemist's shop. On account of its purity the price is high. But sulfur in lumps are cheap and easily procureble from the local markets. Pulverise the lumps and seive the stuff through the fine mesh. It can be applied in a dust form against mites and mildews.

## Blood Meal

It contains 11-13 per cent of nitrogen. Besides 1-2 per cent of phosphoric acid is also available. Nitrogen in plenty becomes readily available from this manure. It is very good for top dressing.

Collect clotted blood (fresh) from the slaughter house and boil it for 3-4 hours. Then get it dry in the sun or in a drier. Pulverise the staff before use.

## Fish Meal

Dry fish or fish waste on drying can be used as a good manure. The analysis is N-P-K 6:5:0 + Calcium 5. Partially decomposed fish can also be used as manure. Put dry fish in a moist condition in a pit for few weeks. Then take it out and break the lumps before use.

Take equal parts of *neem* cake and dry fish waste and mix them together. Put it in a pit in a moist condition for a few weeks. Then take it out and break the lumps before use. Analysis N-P-K 5:5:1 + calcium 5.

## Tobacco Ash

Tobacco ash is a very good source of potash which can be used for the pot plants. Burn dry tobacco stems into white ashes. Collect the stuff in a container for use when needed. The tobacco ash deposited in an ash tray can also be used as a potash fertilizer. The tobacco for cigarette is prepared from the tobacco leaves. Therefore it does not contain as much potash as the ashes from the stem do.

# *Appendix C*

## SEEDSMEN

1. National Seeds Corporation Ltd.
   6, Marquess street, Calcutta-16
2. West Bengal Seeds Corporation Ltd.
   4, Gangadhar Babu Lane, Calcutta-12.
3. B. K. Roy Pvt. Ltd.
   4, Bankshal Street, Calcutta-1.
4. The Agri. Horticultural Society.
   1, Alipur Rd. Calcutta-27.
5. Bankim Prasad Ghosh & Co.
   Belur Station Rd. Bally, Howrah.
6. Amtala Seed Store
   P.O. Bishnupur, 24 Parganas (S)
7. Argosy
   97 Jaswant Place
   Chanakypuri, New Delhi-21.
8. Sungrow Seeds Pvt. Ltd.
   C-33 New Sabji Mandi, Azadpur, New Delhi.

9. Nagpur Beej Bhander
   2, Subhas Rd, Nagpur, Maharastra.

10. Pocha Seeds Pvt. Ltd.
    Solapur Bazar, Pune, Maharastra

11. Ghosh and Co. Ltd.
    Kali Building. Jorhat, Assam.

12. Mesina Been Pvt. Ltd.
    Tejpur Rd. Samastipur, Bihar.

13. The Faizabad Seed Co.
    Faizabad, U.P.

14. L.R.Brothers
    Clock Towers, P.O. Saharanpur, U.P.

15. Pratap Nursery & Seed Stores
    Premnagar, Dehra Dun (U.P.)

16. Kumaun Nursery
    Ramnagar, Nainital. U.P.

17. India Hoby Centre Pvt. Ltd.
    781 (1/155) Mount Rd.
    Chennai, Madras-2.

18. Cuttack Nursery
    Cuttack-9, Orissa.

19. Rourkela Seed Suppliers
    225, Ispat Market, Rourkela-5.

20. Indo-American Hybrid Seeds,
    Banasankari, Stage-2, Bangalore-90.

21. Naolakha Agencies
    Krishi Bhawan, Bhawani gate, Pune-42

22. Capital Seed House
    Haveli Bagh, Khulna, Bangladesh

23. Department of Horticulture
    B.G. Panth Agricultural Institute, Nainital, U.P.

24. Department of Horticulture
    Tamil Nadu Agricultural University.
    Coimbatore, Tamil Nadu.

25. N. S. C. Ltd. Beej Bhawan
    Pusa Complex, New Delhi-12

26. Central Potato Research Institute, Simla,
    Himachal Pradesh.

27. Central Tuber Crops Research Institute.
    I C A R, Trivundrum - 10.

28. Panth Agricultural University,
    Panthnagar, Nainital, U.P.

29. Vegetable Research Station
    Kalyanpur, U.P.

30. Horticultural Arena
    Kadam Kanan, Jhargram,
    Midnapur, Pin-721507 (Author's farm)

31. Indo-American Exports
    a) Bangalore 604940
    b) Hasi Shivam Chambers
       53, Saiyad Amir Ali Avenue, Calcutta-19,
    c) Ramdas Bhawan, Hill Cart Rd, Siliguri,
       Pin - 734 401.

# *Appendix: D*

## PRESERVATION OF VEGETABLES

Vegetables, like fruits, are preserved specially when they become surplus or very cheap in the market. If the surplus vegetables are preserved the supply can be had in the lean period of production. The processing techniques are drying, freezing, pickling, making candy, *chatny* and treating with preservative chemicals. The canned vegetables are in a great demand in the places whereto fresh vegetables cannot be transported. The army and navy need more such products. A large body of army and navy remains in the distant sea or on the snow-clad mountain being secluded from the main land or the main body of the country's population. The exotic vegetables which cannot be grown in a region or in the country can be available as preserves in tin containers. In the plains of the country fresh asparagus is not available. To meet the demand canned asparagus come to the market of the plains.

### Preserve by Drying

The Vegetables like cabbage, cauliflower, radish, morioga stick can be preserved by the simple process of drying and putting in poly bags or poly pouches.

Cut the vegetables as usual for cooking. Dry them in the sun. The area where the dry spell prevails in most part of the year preserving vegetable in this process in feasible. The main principle being to dehydrate the vegetable to protect it from rotting. The principle is adopted in the different methods to preserve vegetables in the processing industry as well as in the household processing. The hot dry sun and the hot wind of summer are exploited for this purpose. The Vegetables preserved in this process are soaked in water for half an hour before cooking. On soaking the characteristics of freshest is resumed to a great extent.

In South India, vegetable banana is sliced and dried in the sun to preserve it for the lean period of supply. In Punjab radish is sliced and a string is passed through the slices to make a garland, which get dried in the very dry weather of the region. Not only radish, cauliflower is also preserved in this way. In the food processing industry vegetable is dried in the dehydrator which are available in the market. Both humidity and temperature can be controlled in the dehydrator. Therefore, the process is very effective and useful. The preserves of potato, onion, pea, cauliflower, and lady's finger are available in packets in the market.

## Onion

It is cut into small pieces and treated with 5 per cent brine for 10 minutes. Then it is dried in the mechanical drier for 12-23 hours.

## Potato

It is peeled and cut into small pieces. Then it is treated with potassium metabisulphate solution. Then it is put into boiling water for only 2-5 minutes. Water is drained off and the potato pieces are dried in 60ø-65ø for 7-8 hours.

## Pea

Take out the peas from the pods. Put then in boiling water for 2-3 minutes. On cooling peas are dried in 70øC for two hours. It should not contain more than 5 per cent of moisture. In this stage, the processed vegetable is packed in aluminum foil pouches.

Cauliflower: It is cut into pieces and treated with 50 per cent sodium sulphite. The steam is applied for 5 minutes. Dry the vegetable in 60 °C till its moisture content goes below 3 per cent.

## Lady's Finger

It is processed like cauliflower.

## Preserve by Freezing

Vegetables can be preserved in the cold storage for a long time as it is done in case of fruits like apple, orange, pear etc. At present, potato and cabbage are thus preserved until the new crops of the next season come to the market.

## Pickling

Vegetables like cauliflower, turnip, carrot, chilli, capsicum, bamboo sprouts, green jack are used in making pickle for preservation. Some vegetable like roselle, carambola, dillenia, karouda etc. are used in making pickle in the conventional process. But the common vegetables can be preserved by using vinegar, lime juice, tamarind pulp etc. The juice of sour orange is considered very useful to preserve vegetable.

Vegetables are cut into pieces as usual. Then put them in steam for 5 minutes. On cooling put the vegetable in the jar containing the juice of sour orange. The juice will be sufficient to cover the vegetable. After a week or so add 10 per cent salt and other spices to taste. If a little vinegar is added pickle thus preserved can be kept for a long time.

## Vegetable Candy

The candy of ash gourd (*Petha*) is very popular. It is known as *petha* in the market. It is also used in making cakes and few other confectionery articles. The ripe ashgourd is cut into small cubes. They are treated with lime water for 15 minutes. Then immersed in sugar solution (syrup). Next day, get the syrup and the cubes separated. Add some sugar in the syrup and boil to get the concentration as before. Again immerse the cubes in the syrup. The process will be repeated for a number of times until the concentration of syrup is not lowered.

## Tomato Sauce

Cut the well ripe vegetable into pieces. Remove the seeds. Then cook the vegetable adding salt, onion, garlic, chilli, sugar, vinegar and other spices to suit the taste until the volume is reduced to the half. Then fill the bottles with the sauce and keep than air tight. In the food processing industry, the bottles with sauce are pasteurized in autoclave. This process makes the product germ-free which is essential for preserving for a long time. But the housewives put the bottles in their refrigerators.

## Chemical Process of Preservation

By using chemicals the housewives can preserve easily. If the cost of bottles is not taken into account one kilogram of vegetables can be preserved by spending only 50-70 paise. Cauliflower, turnip, phuti pea etc. can be preserved by using chemicals.

Make a solution of the following chemicals.

Salt .................................................. 50 g

Potassium metabisulphite ................ 1 g

Glacial acetic acid............................ 12 g

Cut the vegetable into pieces. In case of peas take out the beads from the pods. Immerse the vegetables in the above solution contained in a jar. The quantity of the solution will be just to immerse the vegetables. Close the lid of the jar as usual. If the jars are placed in a cool place the vegetable will maintain their colour and favour for a long time. The taste of the vegetable will be a bit sour as if they were preserved in vinegar. It should be borne in mind that glacial acetic acid is a short of vinegar.

In salad, the vegetable from the jar can directly be used. But for cooking wash them in cold water for several times. But to do it quickly use hot water. A portion of the vegetable can be taken out from the jar. But the empty place should be filled with the solution.

## Preserving Onion

Immature onion is a good vegetable. It is not so pungent. For this reason, it is liked by many. It can be preserved well easily and cheaply.

Remove the base and the crown, and also the outer scale. Kept the bulbs intact. Immerse them in vinegar (8%) contained in a jar. Close the lid and put in a cool place.

# Appendix: E

## SOWING CALENDAR

Most vegetables are season-bound. Therefore, for their good production they must be grown in their respective seasons.

| | |
|---|---|
| April-May | Bottle goard, Cucumber, Pumpkin, Ash gourd, Ribbed goard, Radish (Kharif crop), Elephant foot, Taro, Giant Taro, Yam. |
| May-June | Bottle gourd, Pumpkin, Cucumber, Teasle gourd, Bitter goard, Tinda, Ash gourd, Snake goard, Brinjal, Chilli, Papaya, Vegetable banana, Cow Pea, Indian sorrel, Lady's finger, *Poi* Amaranthus, Ribbed goard etc. |
| June-July | Eddoe, Sweet Potato, All the vegetables mentioned for May-June sowing. |
| July-August | Dolichos bean, Tomato (*Kharif* crop), Cauliflower (`Early Patua', `Pusa Early'). |
| August-September | Cabbage (Early varieties), Cauliflower, Tomato, Beet, Spinach etc. |
| Spet.-October | Cabbage, Cauliflower, Beet, Spinach Tomato, Kinol-Khol, Beans. |
| Octo.-November | Cabbage, Cauliflower, Beet, Tomato, Knol-Khol, Beans, Brussel sprouts, Broccoli, Kale, Pea, Parwal, Kandri, Water melon, Musk melon, *Phuti, Kakri,* |

| | |
|---|---|
| | Tomato, Brinjal, Chilli, Capsicum, Radish, Carrot, Turnip, Parsnip, Celery, Onion, Shallot, Lettuce, Parsnip, Celery, Onion, Shallot, Lettuce, Leafy onion, Leek, Garlic, Parssley, Coriander, Cress, Mint, Spinach, Fenugreek, *Piring*, Potato. |
| Nov.-December | All the vegetables mentioned for the period of Oct.-Nov., Squash. |
| Dec.-January | Tomato, Sweet Potato (as *Rabi* crop), For the early crop of all summer vegetables (Germinated seeds should be sown). |
| February-March | Water spinach (Kalmi sag), Pumpkin, Cucumber, Bottle gourd (Rabi crop), Water melon, Must melon, *Phuti, Kakri*, Radish (*Rabi* crop), *Poi*, Amaranthus, Okra, Bitter gourd, Ribbed gourd. |